Some day I shall make camp at that place:—
so far, so lone upon the empty plains!—
close to that ground there shall be camp for me.
Low against the brightness of the west
lies the long Coast Range, cut clear
from Diablo, faint in the north to the blue southward spur
that ending in mirage hides Coalinga.
There is bending prairie grass at that place, and swales
where little pools have dried,
white-diamonded in rings of alkali.
And two good saddle horses I will have,
and a lean brown cowboy there to ride with me;
and I will stay awhile, easily, and dream
in that place with the sun and meditate
upon the generous largeness of this earth,
the nameless intimacy of grass and sky;
upon the confident placidity of animals
and the wonder of cool water
drawn up from the deep solid ground,—and then—
the wailing of coyotes in the night;—
all these, and the innumerable stars.

—Maynard Dixon

PICTURING CALIFORNIA'S OTHER LANDSCAPE

This book is being published in conjunction with the exhibition "Picturing California's Other Landscape: The Great Central Valley," organized by The Haggin Museum, Stockton, California. We are extremely grateful to those whose generous contribution made the exhibition, the book, and associated educational programs possible.

The Parker and Florence Holt Trust made a significant contribution that has underwritten a large part of this entire effort.

Other major contributors
The College of Agricultural and Environmental
    Sciences, University of California, Davis
California Council for the Humanities
Candelaria Foundation
Helen and John Talbot

Patrons
The Modesto Bee
Great Valley Center

Friends
Land O'Lakes

PICTURING CALIFORNIA'S OTHER LANDSCAPE: THE GREAT CENTRAL VALLEY

Edited by Heath Schenker

THE HAGGIN MUSEUM • STOCKTON, CALIFORNIA
HEYDAY BOOKS • BERKELEY, CALIFORNIA

Publisher's Cataloging-in-Publication
(Provided by Quality Books, Inc.)

Picturing California's other landscape : the Great Central Valley /
    edited by Heath Schenker. — 1st ed.
        p. cm.
        ISBN: 1-890771-25-2

        1. Central Valley (Calif. : Valley) in art—Exhibitions.
        2. Central Valley (Calif. : Valley)—Maps. I. Schenker, Heath.
        II. Haggin Museum (Stockton, Calif.)

    N8214.5.U6P53 1999
    760/.044997945/07479455   QBI99-887

COVER PAINTING: Michael Tompkins, *Along Highway 5*.
BACK COVER PHOTOGRAPH: Heath and Phoebe Schenker,
    Picturing Yolo County.
FRONTISPIECE, PLATE 1: Maynard Dixon, *Approaching Storm*, 1921.
Oil on canvas, 16 by 20 in. Fresno Metropolitan Museum.

COVER AND INTERIOR DESIGN: Toki Design, San Francisco

Orders, inquiries, and correspondence should be addressed to:
Heyday Books
P.O. Box 9145
Berkeley, CA 94709
510/549-3564; Fax 510/549-1889
heyday@heydaybooks.com

Printed in Singapore by Imago

10 9 8 7 6 5 4 3 2 1

FULL VALUE BRAND

SHIPPER
TULARE COUNTY CITRUS FRUIT EXCHANGE.

No. III

STECHER LITHO CO. ROCHESTER. N.Y.

RESEARCH FOR THIS PROJECT HAS TAKEN ME TO MUSEUM BASEMENTS, ARTISTS' STUDIOS, BUSINESSES, STORAGE rooms, local galleries, historical societies, libraries, and archives. Looking back through the thick, black notebook in which I have scribbled so many notes and phone numbers over the past few years, I find many people deserving thanks for their help.

First, thanks to all the artists who have generously and enthusiastically supported this idea, both with their art and with their time. If this project had a catalyst, it was Michael Tompkins's painting (on the cover of this book), which vividly demonstrated the power of visual representation to me a few years ago, making me see "Dutch" landscapes everywhere as I rode my bicycle through the countryside of Yolo County. Other artists who helped greatly include Esteban Villa, who took me and my daughter on a memorable tour of Sacramento two years ago; Dick Meisinger, who provided an introduction to a group of Sacramento-area photographers who met on Friday nights at The Dark Room; Shelly Stone and David Koeth, who opened doors in Bakersfield; and Ellen Van Fleet, with whom I have enjoyed painting the valley landscape from vantage points along its backroads.

I want to thank Tod Ruhstaller, Director of The Haggin Museum, for his immediate and enthusiastic response to the exhibit proposal and for his unflagging support throughout this project, as well as the staff at The Haggin Museum, particularly Susan Benedetti and Karen Jahnke Barila. Staff at other museums also assisted a great deal, particularly Carey Caldwell, Curator of History, Oakland Museum; Jeff Nickell, Lead Curator, Kern County Museum; and Jan Driesbach, Curator, Crocker Art Museum.

For his enthusiasm, commitment, and sense of humor, thanks to Malcolm Margolin of Heyday Books, without whom there would be no book. Thanks also to Julianna Fleming for expert editing. For research assistance, thanks to Diane Cary and Jan Goggans. Others who consulted generously on this project include Gerald Haslam, Stan Yogi, David Mas Masumoto, Price Amerson, and Tere Romo. Michiko Toki of Toki Design, San Francisco, made this book a work of graphic art. Many librarians have helped with the research, especially Gary Kurutz, Special Collections Librarian of the California State Library, and John Skarstadt, Pam Pogojeff, and David Lundquist of Shields Library, University of California, Davis.

I dedicate this book to my parents, Eric and Barbara Massey, to whom I owe everything, including my first experience of the Central Valley as a series of pungent, night-time odors: fruit blossoms, tomatoes, cows. My husband, Marc, and daughters, Yael, Phoebe, and Hilary, are my inspiration always.

Heath Schenker, June 1999

CALIFORNIA

10

IN 1996, PROFESSOR HEATH SCHENKER WROTE TO ME AND PRESENTED THIS INTRIGUING PROPOSAL: Would The Haggin Museum be interested in collaborating with her in assembling an exhibition of paintings, photographs, commercial art, and maps to demonstrate and explain the many ways California's Great Central Valley has been depicted over the past 150 years? The answer was yes, and for a number of reasons.

Since opening in June of 1931, The Haggin Museum's mission has been to foster an interest in and appreciation for the fine arts and history. Its art collection focuses upon late nineteenth and early twentieth century European and American paintings and includes some excellent examples of works by Albert Bierstadt, William Keith, and Julian Wallbridge Rix. Its history displays explore the pasts of California, San Joaquin County, and Stockton through exhibits about the state's Native people, the city's gold rush beginnings, the development of regional agriculture, and the contributions of the area's culturally and ethnically diverse population. Additionally, its library and archives house an extensive collection of photographic and cartographic materials.

Three years after Professor Schenker's initial correspondence, The Haggin Museum will observe the sesquicentennial of California's gold rush with the exhibition "Picturing California's Other Landscape: The Great Central Valley." Its art and history duality forms a perfect complement to the museum's mission and collections, just as this book serves as a perfect complement to that exhibition. But unlike the exhibition, which is a temporary phenomena, the images and essays in this volume provide insights that will enable readers to view the Central Valley from a number of new perspectives for years to come.

The museum's Board of Trustees extends its sincere appreciation to Professor Schenker for selecting the Haggin to help present this valuable examination of an all too often ignored aspect of California—the Great Central Valley.

Tod Ruhstaller, Director, The Haggin Museum

PLATE 3: Allan Cartography of Medford, Oregon, prepared for Raven Maps and Images, using base materials from the United States Geological Survey. *California,* 1992. Lithograph, 34 by 49 in. Collection of Heath and Marc Schenker.

PAINTINGS AND SCULPTURE

THE IMAGES IN THIS BOOK WILL COME AS A revelation to many viewers. In a state celebrated for its scenery, the Central Valley landscape has suffered from a lack of presence in the popular imagination. While the dramatic landscapes of the Sierra Nevada and the coast are seen as places of scenic value, the vast interior valley is widely regarded as the featureless terrain one drives through to get somewhere else. The mountains, rugged northern seashore, golden southern beaches, even the exotic desert have been appropriated as symbols of California culture in promotional literature, in the movies, and on television. By contrast, the Central Valley landscape occupies a kind of void in the center of California and in California culture at large.[1]

The focus of these images is a 450-mile long stretch between Bakersfield and Redding—a broad, flat valley sandwiched between the Sierra Nevada and the Coast Range. Although the valley may be a conceptual void in California culture, it is rapidly filling up. In terms of population, it is one of the fastest growing regions in the state, as housing tracts encroach upon the agricultural landscape. But valley newcomers often have little understanding of regional history and little aesthetic appreci-

PLATE 4: Albert Bierstadt, *Sacramento Valley in Spring*, n.d. Oil on canvas, 55 by 85 in. The Fine Arts Museums of San Francisco.

ation of the local landscape. "Picturing California's Other Landscape: The Great Central Valley" fills in that blank space with a collection of visual images.

The visual arts have long played an important role in helping people see and understand places in visual and aesthetic terms. Visual images build relationships between people and the places where they live; they transform land into landscape. The various methods of visual representation collected in this exhibit—cartography, painting, photography—all represent different ways of seeing and representing the landscape of the Central Valley. Each of these methods of representation has its own rules and goals, yet they share the ability to shape the visual identity of a place. Once we have seen a map, towns take on locations in relation to each other and in relation to topographic features; rela-

tive distances make more of an impression, fixed in our minds in terms of the map. Similarly, a painter's vision of the landscape can shape the way a place looks to us, make us notice certain things, look for certain features, show us a different point of view.

How should viewers approach these images? The short answer is: this is a collection of aesthetic objects that can be appreciated in purely visual terms. The images—maps, paintings, lithographs,

Heath Schenker

and photographs—were all crafted for this purpose, to be visually arresting and interesting. They all have "the power to stop the viewer in his or her tracks, to convey an arresting sense of uniqueness, to evoke an exalted attention."[2] Viewers can enjoy this as a visual feast, select favorites, compare and contrast various images, measure each one against personal experience of the valley landscape.

The longer answer is: this is a visual record of the vast interior valley of California. These images document physical changes to the region as it has been transformed by agriculture, industry, and successive waves of people who have entered the valley looking for a better life during the past 150 years. Many of the images show political and social conditions, as well as topographical features

The picturesque sensibility determined which subjects nineteenth-century American artists chose to represent. Some places were more worthy of representation in a painting than others.

unique to the region. Each image depicts the Central Valley at a particular moment; collectively, they show changes over time.

However, this visual history is selective and subjective. These images *really* show how the valley has been perceived over time by visual artists. The artists responded to what they saw, but they saw through certain perceptual frameworks, reflecting fluctuating interests of the art world, which in turn

reflect philosophical, religious, and political ideas circulating in the culture at large. These frameworks have shaped how artists see the land, how they compose views, and what styles of representation they choose.

This essay explores some of the perceptual frameworks that have influenced visual artists in the valley, particularly painters. Other essays in this book explore maps, photographs, and lithographs in various contexts. Statements by the visual artists themselves are included to give additional information about the process of constructing the Central Valley landscape visually and aesthetically. But the images themselves are the most effective means for stimulating a dialogue about the Central Valley landscape and bringing it into focus as a subject.

THE PICTURESQUE

Paintings and drawings of the Central Valley produced in the nineteenth century show the influence of a popular nineteenth-century aesthetic: the picturesque. The picturesque was a landscape aesthetic from Europe that categorized scenery according to its suitability for representation in a picture. A picturesque landscape "was characterized by irregularity of form, rough texture, pleasing variety, and contrasts of light and dark. Its effect was to arouse curiosity and interest, and therefore provide delight."[3] Many of the painters who worked in the Central Valley during this time had trained and studied in Europe. Steeped in European aesthetics, they adapted these ideas to American scenery.

The Reverend William Gilpin had introduced the picturesque to the English at the end of the eighteenth century. His enthusiasm for picturesque scenery embraced both landscape paintings and the land itself. Gilpin's guidebooks sent hordes of middle-class, English travelers on a quest for picturesque scenery throughout the British Isles. Formerly, landscape appreciation in England had been the province of an English aristocracy whose taste was formed on continental tours, but Gilpin promoted the picturesque as an aesthetic that could be applied to the English countryside.

Educated Americans adopted the British enthusiasm for the picturesque and began to apply it to the American landscape in the nineteenth century. The picturesque spread among an expanding American middle class by means of books and periodicals that published travelers' accounts of remote areas of the United States, particularly the West. Visual artists produced engravings of picturesque scenery to accompany these travelogues. *Picturesque America,* a serialized book offered by subscription, was published between 1872 and 1874. Edited by William Cullen Bryant, it reached a wide audience and helped to fix landscape imagery in the American

consciousness. *Picturesque California,* edited by John Muir, followed in 1888. These publications, and others like them, created an American audience for picturesque landscapes.

The picturesque sensibility determined which subjects nineteenth-century American artists chose to represent. Some places were more worthy of representation in a painting than others. The picturesque directed artists' attention first at nature. Mountains and water were popular subjects because they emphasized the sublimity of nature, inspiring a sense of awe in viewers. However, the picturesque was an aesthetic that accommodated detail as well as grandeur. Picturesque qualities could be found in the shape and texture of a tree trunk, as well as in a distant view of snow-capped peaks or a precipitous waterfall.

The influence of the picturesque shows in the landscape images produced by nineteenth-century artists in the Central Valley. River and water scenes were the most common subjects in that period. Rivers served as a regular means of transportation for nineteenth-century travelers, so many artists actually saw the land from river corridors. Artists appreciated river views because they offered some topographical variation in the otherwise flat landscape—picturesque sensibility found flatness dull. Painters often focused on reflective qualities of water, particularly at sunset or sunrise. Light was

carefully manipulated to highlight certain landscape features and to create a transcendent mood (Plate 12). Artists were also attracted to the region's great valley oaks for their irregular and shapely habit, the rough texture of their bark, and their venerable age, which inspired awe (Plate 11).

Cities and towns, and even industry, could also be appreciated in picturesque terms. Most appealing were towns that boasted dramatic settings, had historic buildings, or displayed the requisite picturesque qualities of variety and unevenness. Central Valley towns, mostly flat and new, appear infrequently in nineteenth-century landscape paintings. However, Albertus Browere's painting, *View of Stockton* (Plate 7), depicts that city picturesquely by giving prominence to the river and showing the buildings as an irregular outline in the distance. William Coulter's painting, *Stockton Channel* (Plate 15), does the same, bathing the port in a sublime light and emphasizing a jagged and irregular skyline by dramatic use of smoke-stacks, ship masts, and trees. In William Hahn's painting, *Sacramento Railroad Station* (Plate 9), the movement of the crowd, the smoke of the train, and the lively horses create a picturesque tension. Trains were an acceptable subject because they symbolized the technological sublime.[4] With their speed, trains offered passengers a thrill akin to that offered by sublime natural scenery.

A picturesque sensibility guided not only the selection of a subject, but also the composition of a picture, or, the arrangement of elements within a particular landscape view. Vistas were usually arranged into foreground, middle-ground, and distance. Often a scene was framed by a coulisse of trees. Nature loomed large in picturesque views, while evidence of human civilization was usually a distant element. These compositional techniques,

along with the subject preferences of picturesque artists, could produce remarkably similar views of very different places. A river scene in California could look much like a river scene in the Hudson River Valley, for example.

A powerful aesthetic, the picturesque view became linked to Manifest Destiny. By rendering the unknown in familiar terms, it figuratively subdued new territory in a colonial age. The following description of the Central Valley, taken from *Picturesque America*, describes the landscape in terms of Manifest Destiny:

> Beyond the river stretches the interminable prairie, where the fields of harvested wheat lie wrapped in slumber; and not a single ranch gives even a token of life. The light, stealing upon the broad shadows, first touches the tops of the prairie-wagons, and glorifies the brass ornaments of the patient mules. Then, making more and more progress, it shines upon the broken and fragmentary huts that Indians have left, and at last, in full glory of splendor, brings out the yellow of the cultivated fields and the coarse brown of the sandy soil.[5]

In this passage, the light of "progress" spreads across the land. Picturesque paintings also depicted the light of progress. For example, the painting *Harvest Time* (Plate 5), by William Hahn, bathes a wheat harvest in golden light, as though blessed by fortune. Children play innocently in the foreground, suggesting citizens of the future. The ease and "naturalness" of this picture legitimizes American colonization in the Central Valley. The grand scale of the painting makes it a history painting, a document in the heroic taming of the wilderness.

Picturesque landscape paintings often appeared to be disinterested representations of nature, promoting the idea that the aesthetic or philosophic enjoyment of nature was free and available to all. In the nineteenth-century United States, this idea gained power from its association with Transcendentalist philosophy. Landscape images were seen to embody certain religious and moral values, and the transcendental experience of nature was seen as universal. The picturesque aesthetic made the land seem something everyone could enjoy—at least visually.

In celebrating the *natural* landscape, however, the picturesque sensibility could obscure other ways of seeing by leaving components out of the picture. For example, picturesque views rarely included Native Americans, or rendered them small, as if part of the natural scenery. Paintings in this exhibit by Native American artists depict the nineteenth-century Central Valley landscape from a very different point of view. Dal Castro's painting, *Maidu Walk* (Plate 31), looks back on an event in 1863, when the Maidu people living on the eastern

edges of the Central Valley were marched past the Marysville Buttes, a sacred site of their ancestral spirits, to the Round Valley Reservation on the north coast. Many died along the way. The Central Valley landscape serves as a setting for this atrocity in Castro's painting. The Marysville Buttes, rising out of the vast, sun-baked prairie, contrast strikingly with the line of people winding across the valley under the malevolent eye of a whip-cracking overseer. This painting puts pre-colonial people back into the picture, challenging the picturesque view that focused on the landscape as though it were empty, just waiting for settlement. It replaces the divine light of progress with a hot, searing sunlight. No coulisse of trees softens the foreground; the viewer is plunged forcefully into the scene.

Nature loomed large in picturesque views, while evidence of human civilization was usually a distant element.

Frank LaPena notes that, according to Native American traditions, land in the Central Valley was not something to look at or picture or even to own; it was something inseparable from humanity and the sense of self. LaPena views the Central Valley through the frame of American traditions such as storytelling, music, and dance. Dancers in his painting, *Hesi Spirit* (Plate 34), take the landscape as their subject and inspiration; they express the land itself. Another Native American artist, Frank Day, painted stories embodied for Maidu people in the various flora, fauna, landforms, and rivers in the valley. His painting, *Fish Dancer* (Plate 28), shows a man in the skin of a sturgeon; man and fish are inseparable, one inside the other.

These Native American artists complicate the picture of the Central Valley landscape in the nineteenth century, making the point that the landscape was, and remains, subject to controversy. A strong connection exists between a landscape as represented in pictures and the way a culture values and relates to the land. The landscape, whether described verbally or expressed in a picture, "is a process by which social and subjective identities are formed—a medium of exchange between the human and the natural, the self and the other."[6]

THE AMERICAN SCENE

In the 1930s, artists in the United States began to look at the American landscape through a new frame. Shifting their attention from scenes of transcendent nature, they discovered aesthetic potential in the landscapes of everyday experience. This new subject became an art movement: American Scene Painting.

This shift in art came at a time when the United States sought to detach itself from European entanglements, both politically and culturally. It was also the period of the Great Depression. In response to these crises, seeking to develop a new aesthetic to express American social and political ideals, these artists began to focus on uniquely American subjects. "The American Scene was a movement of hope and optimism, of self-recognition and self-glorification—a movement that looked to the future as well as to the past. Complex and contradictory, it represented the fervent wish that America had artistically come of age and that it would now create an art expressive of its own traditions and aspirations."[7]

The American Scene Movement encompassed two quite different factions: regionalism and social realism. Differences between these groups were hotly debated in the 1930s.[8] The regionalists focused on rural American landscapes, celebrating American farm and country scenes as representative of the agrarian roots of American society. The most well known of the regionalists were Grant Wood, Thomas Hart Benton, and John Stuart Curry. The regionalists largely ignored the devastating social effects of the Depression in rural areas. They sought, instead, to depict the life of hard-working farmers, portraying the beauty of the land and evoking a sense of community among rural people.

By contrast, the social realists focused on harsh social conditions in rural areas and labor problems in cities, exacerbated by the Depression. They depicted not only farmland, but also the landscapes of towns and factories, railroad sidings, back lots, and alleys. They showed landscapes of homelessness and poverty. Strong labor and leftist sympathies emerged in their views of the American landscape. The artist who perhaps most exemplified social realism was Ben Shahn. W.P.A. photographers like Dorothea Lange were also social realists.

Both regionalists and social realists focused on aspects of the American landscape formerly underrepresented in art. They brought a more familiar, mundane American landscape scenery to the forefront of public consciousness. The American Scene Movement was unified more by subject than by style, but stylistically the artists in the movement shared a devotion to realism, rejecting abstraction because of its European origins.

In California, a group of painters coalesced during the 1930s and formed a subset of the American Scene Movement. These California Scene painters developed a realist style characterized by broad, loose brushwork and strong colors. Most were watercolorists. They traveled the state in search of suitable subjects to represent the California subset of the American Scene.[9] Some painted the Central Valley, depicting farm life, street life, and river life. They sought to represent the regional landscape of the valley and its characteristic visual qualities. For example, Millard Sheets's painting, *Walnut Creek Canyon* (Plate 19), shows golden hills looming over a small ranch scene. The landscape is sun-baked and bare. The tiny ranch seems to represent a marginal existence. The painting celebrates the glorious color and sensuous curves of the hills that ring the edges of the valley. Barse Miller's painting, *Along the Sacramento River* (Plate 22), shows a sleepy river town. Long shadows and silhouetted figures give this image a somewhat somber mood, suggesting that this is not a scene of prosperity. By contrast, Otis Oldfield's oil painting, *Steamboat Landing* (Plate 21) of steamboats docked at Broderick on the Sacramento River, is cheerful, bright, and colorful. It celebrates the riverboats and the river life they served—a nostalgic tribute to a passing way of life. Oldfield was born in Sacramento, but did not live in the valley as an adult. This painting suggests that his return to the valley must have been somewhat of a sentimental journey.

The California Scene painters produced beautiful, sensuous, idealized images of the Central Valley in the 1930s. By contrast, Dorothea Lange's photographs, produced during the same period, represent a very different point of view. She saw the regional landscape as a backdrop to human suffering. Her most widely reproduced images are portraits of migrant workers, showing the great hardship many experienced in the midst of plenty in the Central Valley. In her photograph, *A Very Blue Eagle, Tranquility Vicinity, Fresno County* (Plate 71), an eagle is shown as a victim of the success of corporate agriculture in the valley, crucified in a landscape devoted to a single-minded purpose— much like the people she often photographed.

The American Scene Movement focused attention on the hinterlands of the United States and made cultural landscapes a suitable subject for art, allowing these landscapes to enter the American consciousness in new ways. The American Scene Movement also paved the way for later visual artists to conceptualize the idea of landscape much more broadly. Social realism in the 1930s had the

The American Scene Movement focused attention on the hinterlands of the United States and made cultural landscapes a suitable subject for art, allowing these landscapes to enter the American consciousness in new ways.

additional effect of stimulating viewers to confront the relationship between landscape and politics.

Chicano art, which appeared several decades later, builds on the foundations of social realism. Mexican muralists Diego Rivera, David Siqueiros, and Jose Clemente Orozco, who helped to develop social realism in the 1930s, served as models for Chicano artists in the 1960s by showing how art could represent political issues. While Cesar Chavez was forming the United Farm Workers in Delano in 1965, Chicano artists in the valley were creating murals, posters, and paintings to address social and political issues and to develop a strong cultural and political identity for Mexican Americans.

Subsequent Chicano artists have added new political meaning to the Central Valley landscape. The farmworker experience—the view from the fields—is a recurring subject in Chicano art. In Malaquias Montoya's painting, *Come Siempre Raza* (Plate 6), skeleton farmworkers dance across a field, waving a UFW flag. Here, the landscape is a scene of political awakening, a wellspring from which Montoya's art of social conscience flows. Daniel DeSiga's iconic painting, *Campesino* (Plate 29), shows the kind of back-breaking field experience that obliterates any aesthetic appreciation of the surrounding landscape. The field is shown as flat and generic. This painting depicts the social alienation that migrant workers experience in a landscape where they feel powerless, have no sense of ownership, and cannot put down roots.

ENVIRONMENTALISM

In the late twentieth century, many artists have come to view the landscape as a scene of environmental as well as social alienation. As mounting scientific evidence shows how human habitation upsets delicate ecological balances, landscape images are framed by knowledge of groundwater and air pollution, loss of habitat, and diminishing natural resources. Some artists, like their predecessors in the nineteenth century, selectively edit the modern landscape, choosing to focus on beauty and avoid conflict. Others see the landscape as a victim of human culture and incorporate the incriminating evidence of environmental degradation in their work.

Environmental Art coalesced as a movement in the 1970s, in tandem with the growing politicization of environmental issues following the first Earth Day. An early environmental artwork by Helen and Newton Harrison focused on the Central Valley landscape, specifically the giant federal and state water projects that dammed, diverted, and channeled water in the region. Called *Meditations on the Sacramento River, the Delta and the Bays at San Francisco* (Plate 26), the Harrisons' environmental artwork was a one-day media blitz, including an exhibit of maps, billboards, posters, graffiti, and radio announcements informing the public about the water projects. It was a performance, a public education project, and a political campaign that challenged the power of agribusiness interests served by the water projects. It added yet another political dimension to the Central Valley landscape.

Agribusiness in the Central Valley has not only impacted the land environmentally, but as the dominant land use, it has also impacted the land visually. The repetition inherent in corporate agriculture creates vast patterns on the land, which are appreciable for their precision, as bands of color, and as bold, geometric forms.[10] The valley's flattened topography is laser-planed to precision; few visual landmarks have survived this leveling, but those left break the monotony of the agricultural patterns with startling impact. Rivers and canals in the valley are dammed and diked in service of agribusiness, but they still offer great visual relief as they meander through the rigid geometry of huge fields. Most importantly, agribusiness in the valley has preserved a sense of vast space, which has become rare and valuable in itself.

Many artists find things to appreciate in the agricultural landscapes in the valley today. The aerial view is particularly striking and seductive. From this perspective, in *River Channel* (Plate 48), Wayne Thiebaud paints the vivid colors of planted fields as well as the rich browns of earth and muddy water. His paintings celebrate the visual beauty of the agricultural landscape, but evince an almost abstract preoccupation with light and paint. Roland Petersen's *Picnic with Four Figures* (Plate 33) also depicts the striking patterns and bold colors of the agricultural landscape, but approaches the subject matter more enigmatically. Lone, faceless figures, gazing out at the fields in

Petersen's picnic scenes, seem alienated in the midst of the rich counterpane. Farmer-painters in the valley, such as Paul Buxman and August Madrigal, are neither alienated nor detached from the agricultural landscape. They show valley agriculture from inside the vineyard and the orchard, delineating each tree and vine with a loving eye (Plates 42, 43).

Still, agribusiness has strong negative associations for many people. In terms of social and environmental issues, the industry has a dismal record, representing the demise of family farms, mechanization of labor, displaced workers, and environmental degradation. Some contemporary artists use irony in depicting the agricultural landscape of the valley. They make reference to the enormous environmental costs of corporate agriculture, but they cannot ignore its aesthetic appeal. Darrell Forney looks, with humor, at the valley's famous (and infamous) water projects. His painting, *Archimedes Screw* (Plate 30), shows an irrigation system under construction, employing archaic devices and with cracks already appearing in the concrete. In *Rice Burn* (Plate 35), Ellen Van Fleet shows beauty in a great mushroom cloud produced from a burning rice field. Robert Dawson focuses on

PLATE 6: Malaquias Montoya, *Come Siempre Raza*, 1993-94. Acrylic and prisma pencil, 22 by 30 in. Collection of the artist.

the devastation of the valley's native ecosystem in an iconic image of a single, desperate tree (Plate 76). Richard Meisinger depicts the interface between the agricultural landscape and burgeoning suburbs in the valley, showing two scrawny, struggling, anthropomorphic saplings at the edge of new lawn, tenuously tethered to life by irrigation tubing (Plate 79). These various images picture the agricultural landscape of the Central Valley as a landscape that is simultaneously compelling and repelling, productive and destructive, beautiful and alienating.

CONCLUSION

Late twentieth-century visual representations of the Central Valley show a far different landscape

These various images picture the agricultural landscape of the Central Valley as a landscape that is simultaneously compelling and repelling, productive and destructive, beautiful and alienating.

from the one depicted by artists 150 years ago. Contemporary artists are more diverse and represent a wider range of viewpoints than their nineteenth-century predecessors, and they show a landscape that is more varied, more complex, and more interesting. They also raise many questions, such as: Who makes images of landscapes, and for whom? Do landscape paintings or photographs represent real places? What makes a landscape

scenic or worthy of representation in a work of art? How do various cultural traditions, the traditions of Native Americans and those brought to the valley by waves of immigrants, lead people to see the Central Valley landscape differently and produce various representations of it? Is this a landscape of equal opportunity? Is this the landscape of the future?

Yet some things about the Central Valley landscape have remained constant throughout its history of visual representation. It remains a spacious, open landscape with great vistas and a big sky, framed on clear days by magnificent mountains. It's still a fertile plain where agriculture flourishes as the dominant industry. Rivers in the valley, although diminished, still offer aesthetic and recreational opportunities. Central Valley towns retain traces of their history in railroad stations, silos, riverfronts, main streets, and tree canopies.

The images in this book document what has changed and what has stayed the same, depicting the Central Valley as a diverse, vibrant, living landscape. Shining a spotlight on California's interior, cutting through the tule fog and the fog of cultural invisibility, these images show a place with a strong regional identity and far more nuances than the views from Highway 5 or 99 can reveal. They might just encourage people to leave those highways and explore some of the valley's backroads, perhaps with cameras and paintbrushes in hand. At the very least, they create a strong presence for the Central Valley landscape in the popular consciousness.

Heath Schenker, guest curator of The Haggin Museum's "Picturing California's Other Landscape" exhibit, is Associate Professor in the Landscape Architecture Program at the University of California, Davis. She has written extensively about landscape history and curated several other exhibits on landscape subjects.

1. Two recent books precede this one in focusing on the Central Valley region: Stephen Johnson, Gerald Haslam, and Robert Dawson, *The Great Central Valley: California's Heartland* (Berkeley: University of California Press, 1993); Stan Yogi, ed. *Highway 99: A Literary Journey through California's Great Central Valley* (Berkeley: Heyday Books and the California Council for the Humanities, 1996).

2. Stephen Greenblatt, "Resonance and Wonder," in Ivan Karp and Steven D. Lavine, eds. *Exhibiting Cultures* (Smithsonian Institution Press, 1991), 42.

3. Sue Rainey, *Creating Picturesque America* (Nashville and London: Vanderbilt University Press, 1994), 28.

4. Ibid., 60.

5. *Picturesque America* (New York: D. Appleton and Company, 1872), 416.

6. W.J.T. Mitchell, *Landscape and Power* (University of Chicago Press, 1994), 1.

7. Mathew Baigell, *The American Scene: American Painting of the 1930s* (New York and Washington: Praeger Publishers, 1974), 18.

8. Mathew Baigell has pointed out, however, that as vocal disputes between these two groups accelerated during the 1930s, differences in their work decreased as regionalists developed more social sensitivity. Ibid., 74.

9. See Gordon T. McClelland and Jay T. Last, *The California Style* (Beverly Hills: Hillcrest Press, 1985); Ruth Lily Westphal and Janet Blake Dominik, *American Scene Painting, California, 1930s and 1940s.* (Irvine, California: Westphal Publishing, 1991).

10. See Allen Carlson, "On Appreciating Agricultural Landscapes," *Journal of Aesthetics and Art Criticism,* 43, No. 3 (Spring, 1985), 301–312.

PLATE 7: Albertus Browere, *View of Stockton*, 1854. Oil on canvas, 20 by 30 in. The Haggin Museum.

PLATE 8: William Smith Jewett, *Hock Farm*, 1852. Oil on canvas, 29 by 40 in. California State Parks Resource Center.

PLATE 12: Julian Walbridge Rix, *Upper Sacramento River*, 1876. Oil on canvas, 30 by 40 in. John Garzoli Gallery.

PLATE 13: William Keith, *Sunset Near Suisun*, ca. 1880–90. Watercolor on paper, 7 ¾ by 12 in. The Oakland Museum.

PLATE 14: Raymond Dabb Yelland, *Sunrise at Tracy*, ca. 1880s. Oil on canvas, 22 by 36 in. The Oakland Museum.

PLATE 15: William Coulter, *Stockton Channel*, 1884. Oil on canvas, 26 by 44 in. The Haggin Museum.
PLATE 16: Thaddeus Welch, *Jewett Ranch*, 1893. Oil on canvas, 49 ¾ by 29 ¾ in. The Kern County Museum.

NEG. #: 24,537 (4x5")

PLATE 17: Arthur Francis Mathews, *Sketches for the Capitol Rotunda, Epoch III: Sutter Mill; Fortune leads the way for caravan; Sacramento River and a steamer on the way to the city and the creation of modern civilization*, ca. 1913. Watercolor on brown paper, 8 by 10 in. The California State Library.

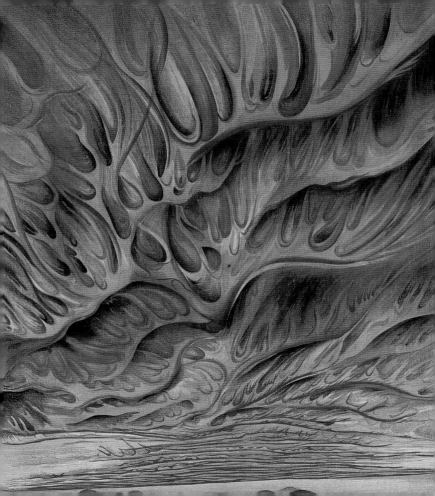

My aim is to create a bowl full of joy/Clear as the sky/Pure as falling cherry petals,/Without worry, without doubt;/Then comes full energy, endless power/And the road to art.—Chiura Obata

PLATE 18: Chiura Obata, *Sunset in the Sacramento Valley*, n.d. (ca. 1928–30). Color woodblock print, 15 5/8 by 10 7/8 in. The Crocker Art Museum.

PLATE 19: Millard Sheets, *Walnut Creek Canyon*, n.d. Watercolor on paper, 16 1/2 by 20 in. Michael Johnson Fine Arts.

PLATE 20: Eugen Neuhaus, *Sutter Buttes*, n.d. Oil on canvas, 30 by 40 in. The Oakland Museum.
PLATE 21: Otis Oldfield, *Steamboat Landing*, 1935. Oil on canvas, 42 by 34 in. Estate of Otis Oldfield.

PLATE 22: Barse Miller, *Along the Sacramento River*, 1941. Watercolor, 21 3/8 by 29 in. The Crocker Art Museum.
PLATE 23: Chee Chin S. Cheung Lee, *The Valley*, 1943. Watercolor, 14 1/2 by 21 1/2 in. Collection of Michael D. Brown.

VALLEY FOG CUTTER   FOR DICK AND HAY NELSON   wiley 76

PLATE 24: Ralph Goings, *Camper Truck*, 1972. Color lithograph, 21 by 32 in. The Crocker Art Museum.

PLATE 25: William Wiley, *Valley Fog Cutter*, 1970. Drypoint etching, 24 by 30 in. Nelson Gallery and the Fine Arts Collection, University of California, Davis.

DYKING   CHANNELING   PUMPING THE WATERS   DIVERTING THE FLOW

OF THE SAN JOAQUIN AT FRIANT   AND THE SACRAMENTO AT THE DELTA

LIMITING THE FLUSHING OF THE DELTA AND THE BAYS   CRISSCROSSING

THE CENTRAL VALLEY WITH DITCHES AND CANALS   WHO DAMMED ALL

THE RIVERS AND MOST OF THE CREEKS THAT FLOW INTO THE DELTA AND

THE BAYS   WHO DAMMED THE SACREMENTO   THE TRINITY   THE MCCLOUD

THE PITT   FALL CREEK   HAT CREEK   COW CREEK   STONY CREEK

BATTLE CREEK   PUTAH CREEK   BUTTE CREEK

WHO DAMMED THE FEATHER ON THE NORTH FORK   THE SOUTH FORK   THE

WEST BRANCH AND ALL THE BRANCHES OF THE YUBA AND THE BEAR

WHO DAMMED OREGON CREEK   CANYON CREEK   FRENCH DRY CREEK   THE

SOUTH FORK AND THE MIDDLE FORK OF THE AMERICAN

WHO DAMMED THE RUBICON   BRUSH CREEK   SILVER CREEK

TELLS CREEK   GERLE CREEK   DRY CREEK

THE MOKELUMNE   THE STANISLAUS   THE TOULUMNE   ANGEL CREEK

CHERRY CREEK   SULLIVAN CREEK   DAMMING AND REDAMMING THE

MERCED   THE SAN JOAQUIN   THE KINGS   THE KAWEAH   THE KERN

—*Helen Mayer Harrison and Newton Harrison, text from* Meditations on the Sacramento River

PLATE 26: Helen Mayer Harrison and Newton Harrison, *Meditations on the Sacramento River, the Delta and the Bays of San Francisco,* 1977. Multi-media installation. Collection of the artists.

PLATE 27: Robert Arneson, *The Palace at 9 a.m.*, 1974. Terracotta and glazed ceramic, 118 by 84 by 24 in. Brian Gross Fine Art.
PLATE 28: Frank Day, *Fish Dancer*, 1973–75. Oil on plywood, 24 by 17 in. Collection of Leigh and Sandra Marymor.

Having seen, painted, and written about common crows in the Sacramento Valley for more than twenty years, I agree with learned ornithologists that the crow may well be the smartest bird in the world. "If men had wings and bore black feathers, few of them would be clever enough to be crows."—Rev. Henry Ward Beecher, nineteenth century

Painting the watercolor, Archimedes Screw, I chose to eclipse past with present for crows in a visual valley hypothesis: the common crow as history, collector, architect, builder, and progenitor of habitats seemingly more natural than we contemporary pioneers appear to be. Corvus brachyrhynchos *were first recorded historically 150 years ago in the Sacramento Valley on a U.S. War Department information mission to build a railroad route from Mississippi to the Pacific Ocean.—Darrell Forney*

PLATE 30: Darrell Forney, *Archimedes Screw*, 1977. Watercolor on paper, 15 by 19 in. Collection of Barbara Zook Caine.
PLATE 31: Dalbert Castro, *Maidu Walk*, 1980. Acrylic on canvas, 24 by 36 in. The Oakland Museum.

PLATE 32: Gregory Kondos, *Sacramento River*, 1981. Oil on canvas, 48 by 60 in. The Crocker Art Museum.

Flying over the valley in small airplanes, I saw what became a source for a sort of compositional field. The earthworks of the farms became a source for this kind of seeing. I watched the clouds floating over the fields and the cast shadows they produced, and that struck me. All my work is about sunlight and shadow, in a sense, those are metaphors for life.—Roland Petersen

PLATE 33: Roland Petersen, *Picnic With Four Figures*, 1983. Mixed media on paper, 22 by 29 1/2 in. Nelson Gallery and the Fine Arts Collection, University of California, Davis.

Art helps to create order through the use of symbols. These symbols help to maintain the connection between traditional and contemporary cultures by reminding us of our responsibility for the way we choose to live, the way we relate our lives to the universal connection of the sacred circle....[Native American] artists work on several artistic levels: conceptual, realistic, and spiritual....
We are told by our elders how the earth and human beings and other living things came to be. This helps us realize and understand how we can develop our own sense about how we fit into the universe, space, and time and how dreams and visions function to help us maintain the quality of life that is beautiful and powerful. Sometimes our art is done through the instruction that we receive in dreams. We may even be given new symbolic forms in our dreams and visions.—Frank LaPena

PLATE 34: Frank LaPena, *Hesi Spirit*, 1984. Acrylic on canvas, 37 3/8 by 49 3/8 in. Collection of Dino Morino.

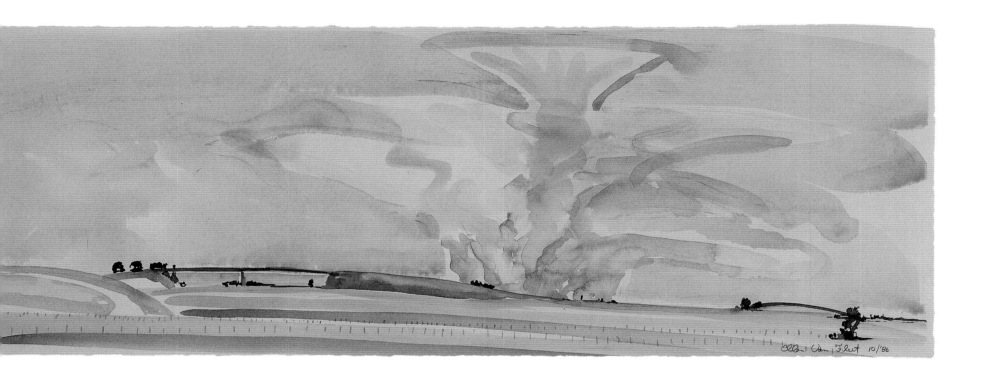

Most landscapes in and around Sacramento are almost flat, so looking up to see a staggered column of smoke rising into the sky creates a fascinating immensity that attracts me. What calls to me I paint.

It is when I think of leaving Sacramento that I look for painting spots because I want to take it with me. I go out and experience it again and again: the hot yellow grass, the oaks, and a roof or two to punctuate the sweep of the horizon. The sky, especially at dawn or dusk, has incredible colors; clouds endlessly varied. The openness and light of this landscape is sensational.
—Ellen Van Fleet

PLATE 35: Ellen Van Fleet, *Rice Burn*, 1986. Watercolor on paper, 11 by 30 in. Collection of the artist.

At this stage of my life, the landscape seems supremely fluid. Human works are in various stages of deliberate destruction or inex-orable decay. Few structural remains survive from the San Diego of my youth. In my current San Joaquin Valley locale, the past quarter century has seen the seeming evaporation of structure after structure, enterprise after enterprise.

When I shift to a vantage of long-term geologic time and ponder an earth that is constantly eroding, being built up, and patiently awaiting the next cataclysm, the above changes, once monumental to me, now seem merely incidental.—Raphael Reichert

PLATE 36: Raphaël Reichert, *"When I was your age...."*, 1989. Metal and found objects, 72 by 28 by 40 in. Collection of the artist.

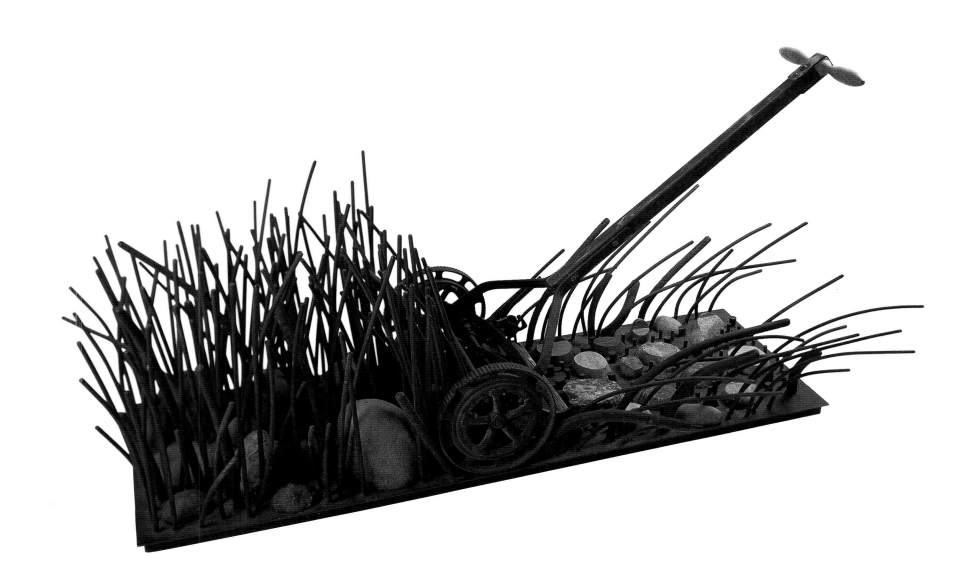

When I came to Davis, it was a real refreshing place to be after Santa Barbara. I thought that it looked like the most boring place in the world. No distractions. A great place to work.

I look at the landscapes around here, especially the industrial ones, and I see paintings of Amsterdam, with the sense of the grandness of sky, that vertical rise of sky. I can't make a moral distinction between virgin landscape and man-altered landscape. The valley is intensely man-altered, so painting it is an excuse to deal with light and the sense of scale, to order things.
—*Michael Tompkins*

PLATE 37: Michael Tompkins, *Along Highway 5*, 1990. Oil on rag board, 5 ¾ by 32 in. Collection of Heath and Marc Schenker.

The Central Valley has annealed my spirit. The hard valley light and its dryness is tough and unforgiving. I am not engaged in a romance. My landscape is state buildings and shopping malls, pizzerias and Southeast Asian restaurants. It is a landscape of violation. Yet there is a landscape. In the mornings before the commuters and sirens and leaf blowers, there is an eerie beauty over our mess.—Fred Dalkey

PLATE 38: Fred Dalkey, *Light Rail Overcrossing*, 1990. Oil on board, 11 by 14 in. Collection of Kathleen Cardwell.

I am a painter increasingly involved with images of the Central Valley. What we have taken for granted for millennia—clean air and water, immensely fertile soil, a balance between the interaction of people and their environment—has become increasingly distorted and degraded.

I cannot easily imagine painting a landscape that does not include the apparent effect of our activities on it. Some of these are visually beautiful, as a blooming orchard or the geometry of row farming. But increasingly, the huge tin sheds, the absence of animals and even people make a flat and dreary image of our countryside.

Part of the function of landscape artists is to provide an historical visual record of their times. I believe this should be done without sentimentality but positively and enthusiastically, recognizing the continuing marvel of nature and at the same time understanding if not accepting the threats to its survival.—Robert Else

PLATE 39: Robert Else, *Workers in a Field*, 1992. Acrylic on canvas, 34 by 48 in. The Solomon-Dubnick Gallery.

The hundreds of miles of soil that surround the lives of Valley dwellers should not be confused with land. What was once land has become dirt, overworked dirt, overirrigated dirt, injected with deadly doses of chemicals and violated by every manner of ground- and back-breaking machinery. The people that worked the dirt do not call what was once the land their enemy. They remember what land used to be and await its second coming.—Cherríe Moraga, Heroes and Saints

PLATE 40: Ester Hernandez, *Heroes and Saints*, 1992. Screen print, 23 by 30 in. Collection of the artist.

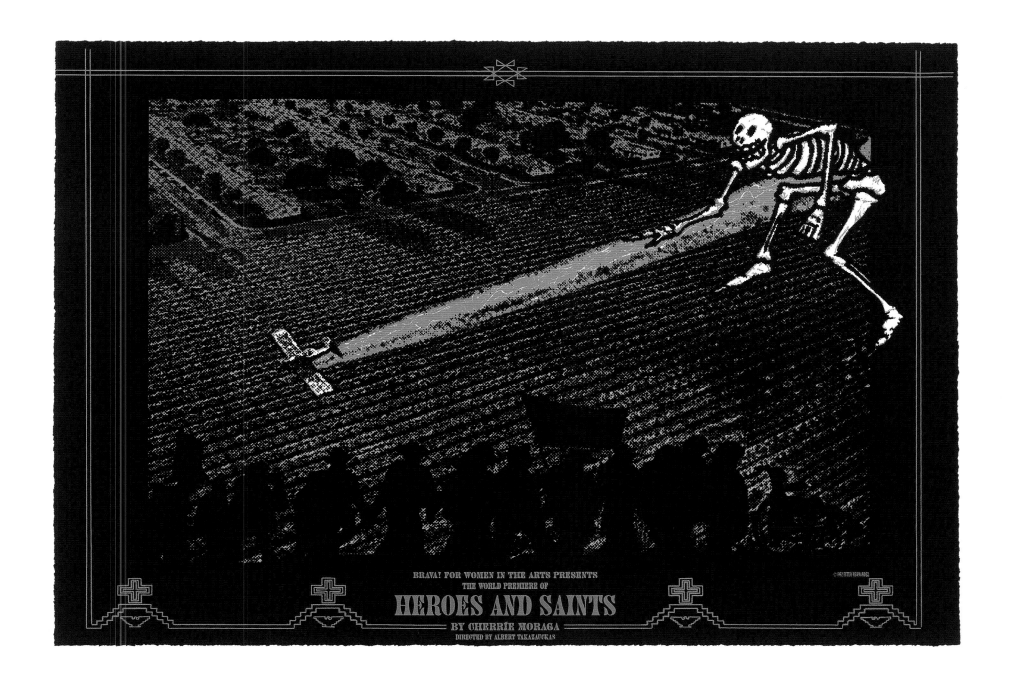

BRAVA! FOR WOMEN IN THE ARTS PRESENTS
THE WORLD PREMIERE OF
HEROES AND SAINTS
BY CHERRÍE MORAGA
DIRECTED BY ALBERT TAKAZAUCKAS

© 1992 ESTER HERNANDEZ

© annabelle simon Cahn

As the harvest finally winds down, and the days grow shorter, I turn my attention again to the unique look and feel of our incredible valley. It is easy to miss the beauty of the San Joaquin when you live in the middle of it. The summer heat and the haze can be stifling, and the fight to hold on to a small family farm can possess every thought. But when the last peach has been picked and the last grapes hauled in, fall finally comes. Shadows lengthen, temperatures cool, and there is once again time to reflect and be thankful for the great valley we call home. It is time again to gather the "visual harvest." There is something simple, truthful, and beautiful in a tray of raisins drying, tractor tire prints in the dirt, and river trees in the near distance. I love painting the vineyards, the orchards, old homes, and the ditches. These are the views from my own farming experiences and those of hundreds of other farmers.—Paul Buxman

PLATE 42: Paul Buxman, *Orchard Along Canal*, 1996. Oil on canvas, 24 by 30 in. Linder/Rempel Collection.

Paul Buxman 1996

My work during the sixties and seventies was constructed in form and non-representational. The landscape came into the picture in the mid-eighties when I spent a sabbatical year on my family's farm. My perception of the valley's agriculture changed completely from when I was growing up here. It too is highly constructed, with beautiful configurations. I retired from teaching in 1986 and now I live on the farm, which was passed on to me, and I have a studio where I work. For me it's wonderful to bring my East Coast perception to the valley where I was born, and my hope is that when I'm gone from this earth my present work will be regarded as significant regional art.—August Madrigal

PLATE 43: August Madrigal, *Sleeping Beauty*, 1996. Oil on canvas, 22 by 34 in. Collection of Susan and Larry Early.

PLATE 44: Vida Hackman, *Panorama Bluffs Burning*, 1996. Etching/pastel, 4 by 35 in. Collection of Kenneth and Vida Hackman.

When I began research for this project, I went to a photo exhibit at the Pear Festival in Courtland. I was so disappointed. In fact I was shocked. The photos were mostly of white farmers. There were no Japanese, no Filipinos, no Mexicans—nothing of them picking, working in the orchards. I can remember all these people in the house where we lived—we lived upstairs. Downstairs was the mess hall—the kitchen and dining room. All the workers would come in for breakfast, lunch, and dinner. My mother was the cook. I can remember all the activity there. I remember the food, the smells, the iceman. Some of the workers would become connected to the family—they were mostly single Japanese men.

I wanted figures in the orchards. I wanted them ghost-like. [These paintings are] a tribute to my family, Japanese-descended people, and those who have worked and cared for this California landscape. Migrant workers have come and gone. There's no record of them whatsoever. The pear orchards look exactly the way they looked when I was five. There's been a lot of people who have picked and worked on those trees. The idea most people have of migrant workers is that they come here to work in the field, then they go back to whatever. You know, when they come here to work, their lives are changed in so many ways. It's not like they come here, make their money, and then go back. Maybe they stay. Maybe they get connected to other people who are here. There are traces of what the land has done to them. And there are traces of what these people have done to the land. We have to look for it.—Hideo Chester Yoshida

PLATE 45: Hideo Chester Yoshida, *In the Delta*, 1996. Mixed media on paper, 36 by 36 in. Collection of the artist.

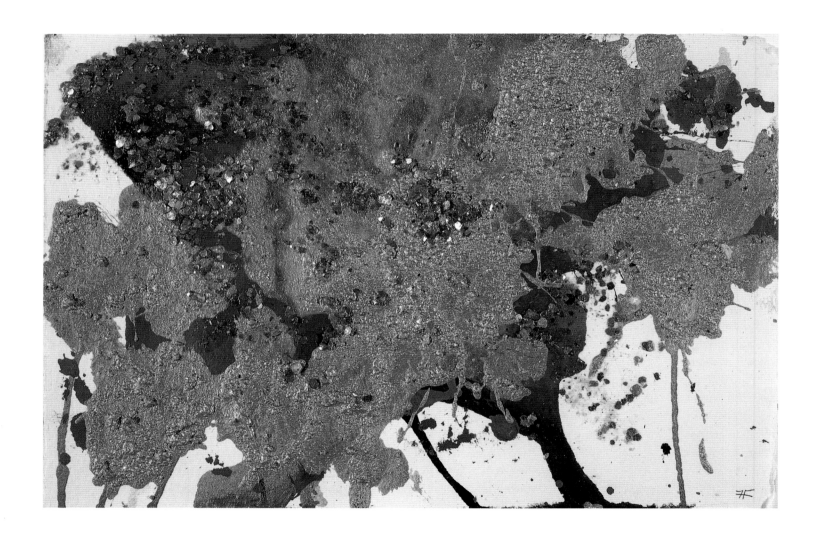

The movement of the river, the sand and endless rocks, the heat, and the openness of it all, the sun and the power of the place came across.

June 25: Yesterday I got to Coloma about 10 a.m. and worked there non-stop until 7 p.m. It was hot, but being by the river made it seem a little cooler. I painted the pieces on the shore while standing in the river. I know the pieces would be considerably different from the ones I painted here on the Res. [sic]

It really was brutal out there and that has surely come across in the work. First the landscape—the blue, the green, and the yellow oxide and then the discovery of gold! And, the pieces began to explode.

July 15: Last Monday I went to Coloma on the American River and did another series of painting on paper. I knew they would be different from the ones I did there the first time—and sure enough they are.

Again, it was so hot! After a period of time you become so hot, it just doesn't make any difference—sort of like picking pears, hops, or tomatoes.—Harry Fonseca

PLATE 46: Harry Fonseca, *The Discovery of Gold in California*, 1997. Mixed media on paper, 8 by 11 in. American Indian Contemporary Arts.

The Chicano barrios of the Great Central Valley—from Bakersfield to Marysville—have always been, from my earliest childhood memories, the center of my creative universe. And the main artery that pumped the blood-line of life and death in and out of that universe was Highway 99. My art, my poetry, and my songs come forth from that experience. I feel at once blessed and burdened to have so much to draw from. Allí está todo. It's all there.—José Montoya

PLATE 47: José Montoya, *The Curandera's Dog*, 1997. Watercolor, 30 by 36 in. Collection of the artist.

The one that I'm working on now has to do with the river and the way in which agricultural patterns relate to the river. A lot of
does have to do with an aerial perspective. But also it's just driving along levees. I've been thinking about and working on that
quite a while without having a lot of things produced. But now I've got fifteen or twenty studies and other works, and I've start
a couple of big ones, which I'm hoping, somehow, will maybe bring together the ideas that interest me—the idea of a river as a
source for agriculture, like the Nile Valley. The big trick is to try to avoid, again, the pictorial aspect of the river. It's such a see
ive enterprise, to paint a river, the reflections, the prettiness of it, and so on.—Wayne Thiebaud

PLATE 48: Wayne Th

MAPS

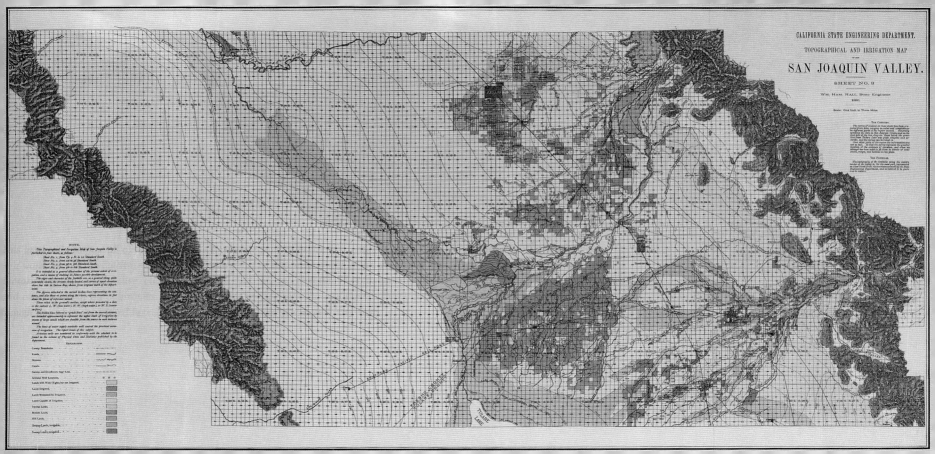

CALIFORNIA STATE ENGINEERING DEPARTMENT.

TOPOGRAPHICAL AND IRRIGATION MAP
OF THE
SAN JOAQUIN VALLEY.

SHEET NO. 9

WM. HAM. HALL, State Engineer.
1886.

Scale: One Inch to Three Miles.

MAPS, LIKE OTHER IMAGES, ARE REPRESENTATIONS of the world that are intended to affect action. Maps not only record visions of a place, but also transform places in line with those visions. Most maps of California's Central Valley have been designed to facilitate the control and exploitation of its land and other resources. The dominant story they tell is that of Euro-American conquest and transformation.

In the nineteenth century, Mexican citizens used *diseños,* or sketch maps, to claim portions of the Central Valley. The 1828 colonization law required *diseños* as part of any petition to the Mexican government for a land grant. *Diseños* have survived for many of the roughly 600 Mexican land grants later confirmed by the U.S. government, about four dozen of which were located in the Central Valley.

The *diseño* for the Larkin Children's Rancho (Plate 50) delineates an area of ten square leagues (44,364 acres) located on the west bank of the Sacramento River in what today are Glenn and Colusa counties. The *diseño* was drawn by one of the Sacramento Valley's most eminent American pioneers, John Bidwell, who produced maps for

PLATE 49: William Hammond Hall, *Topographical and Irrigation Map of the San Joaquin Valley,* 1886. Lithograph, 18 by 25 1/2 in. University of California, Davis/Shields Library.

more than forty Mexican land grants in California.[1] In the case of the Larkin Children's Rancho, he did more than the cartography. He visited the area and picked out the property at the request of Monterey merchant Thomas O. Larkin, the United States Consul to Mexican California from 1844 to 1848.

The *diseño* drawn by Bidwell of the Larkin Children's Rancho contains conventional cartographic elements such as a scale (in varas; one vara equals approximately thirty-three inches) and compass rose. The simple map displays water courses, riparian vegetation, scattered trees, and bits of the Sutter Buttes and Sierra Nevada foothills.

The only cultural features on the map are Native American settlements: *rancherías* Sunu, Sojot, Dacdac, and Queti. Each of these *rancherías* is located within the boundaries of the land grant.

PICTURING THE CENTRAL VALLEY THROUGH MAPS

Despite the fact that the native peoples of Central California were divided into numerous territorially based groups with developed concepts of land ownership and trespass, and despite the fact that Spanish and Mexican law recognized certain native property rights,[2] this map ignored any territorial claim by the inhabitants. On many *diseños* and other early maps of the Central Valley, Native American settlements were treated cartographically like

Robin Elisabeth Datel

trees and rivers and hills—as natural features of the land now belonging to Mexican citizens. Or they were not shown at all, a cartographic assertion of their powerlessness.

Once Mexico ceded California to the United States in 1848, the *diseños* became important documents in the long, convoluted process of sorting out land claims.[3] A missing or inaccurate *diseño* weakened a claim; an authoritative *diseño* legitimized the authority of its maker and user. Bidwell was on hand to testify on behalf of the Larkin Children's claim that the Native American settlements he had located on the *diseño* years before "were then and are now well known points, particularly that called Sojot. At those villages there are almost

The diseños, *sketchy and ambiguous though they were, marked the arrival of a society where real property was privately held, and one where the fantastically unequal distribution of real property was the basis for enormous social inequality.*

invariably found considerable mounds which remain for many years and are noted landmarks....I have no doubt that the land intended to be contained in the map could with its aid be easily identified and located."[4] No trace of irony touched Bidwell's use of Native American mounds as landmarks to substantiate the claims of Mexican land grantees, rather than the (silent) claims of those who had made the mounds years earlier.

The eventual recognition of most Mexican land grant claims by the American government, partly based on cartographic documentation, helped establish the pattern of large holdings that continues to characterize parts of the Central Valley today. The *diseños*, sketchy and ambiguous though they were, marked the arrival of a society where real property was privately held, and one where the fantastically unequal distribution of real property was the basis for enormous social inequality. Huge swathes of the Central Valley became the property of a handful of people.

As *diseños* helped establish the authority of the *rancheros*, so the maps created by the expeditions of John Charles Frémont helped legitimize the claims of the United States to the western reaches of North America (Plate 52). Frémont's father-in-law was Senator Thomas Hart Benton, one of the country's most avid proponents of Manifest Destiny. "Like most of the Topographical Engineers, he [Frémont] was particularly susceptible to projects for national aggrandizement. They worked as part of an institution dedicated to that cause, and in an atmosphere of romantic optimism and absolute belief in the nation's potential."[5]

In March of 1843, Frémont was ordered to survey certain parts of the Great West between the head of the Kansas River and a point on the Columbia River. An important part of the agenda behind these orders was gathering information on Oregon and the Oregon Trail. Nothing was said about California, and even in November 1843, when Frémont turned southward for the journey home, he intended to remain east of the Sierra Nevada and explore the Great Basin. His own explanation for why he decided in January 1844 to cross the mountains into the valley of the Sacramento referred to the poor condition of his animals' feet. Others have suggested that he "could not resist the opportunity to obtain geographical and political information on California."[6]

After a harrowing winter crossing of the Sierra, Frémont and his men followed the American River down out of the mountains. They reached Sutter's Fort on March 8, stayed for about two weeks, and then spent three weeks traveling down the east side of the San Joaquin Valley, probably exiting the valley by way of Oak Creek Pass.

The map that the expedition's cartographer, Charles Preuss, prepared to accompany Frémont's report was "perhaps the most important map of the decade," and it "radically and permanently altered western cartography....The Frémont map was carefully drawn, with its locations adequately checked by astronomical observations. And, for the first time upon a published map it showed the entire area west of the Mississippi as seen by a single party."[7] Frémont's use of scientific instruments and his care

to include only places his own expedition visited and observed (with a couple of exceptions, including the Pacific coastline) added to the map's credibility and legitimacy.

This map became, among other things, an important piece of propaganda for the advocates of Manifest Destiny, as it visually tied together far-flung regions of the West in anticipation of their subsequent political incorporation into the United States. Potential migrants were given the best depictions yet of the lower Sacramento and San Joaquin rivers. In numerous published editions of the report, they read Frémont's enthusiastic descriptions of the climate, soils, rivers, and plant and animal life of the Central Valley. Frémont's map and report helped claim California for the nation by advertising the Central Valley as an opportunity for migrants, who then made that claim a reality.

MAPS SUCH AS THOSE BY BIDWELL AND FRÉMONT (as well as Derby; Plate 53) were representations of the existing Central Valley as seen through the eyes of the mapmakers. With California's statehood and settlement, maps began to portray visions of the valley's future, not just representations of what was already there. Numerous maps proposing rail routes (such as that of the California Pacific Railroad, 1866; Plate 55), new towns and cities, drainage and irrigation schemes, and small farm

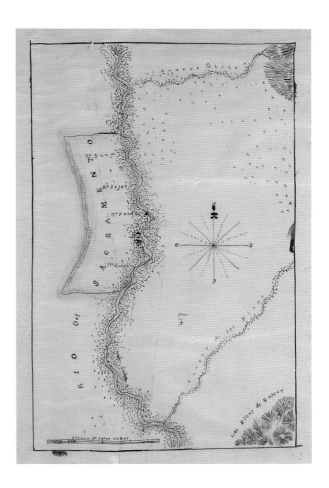

PLATE 50: John Bidwell (attributed to), *Diseño for Larkin Children's Rancho*, 1844. Hand-traced copy of the original, ink and pencil on tracing paper, 7 by 11 in. California State Archives.

subdivisions came quickly. However, these visions could not be realized until the federal government acted to make its vast lands available.

Beginning with the U.S. Rectangular Land Survey in 1851, federal lands in California were surveyed into thirty-six-square-mile townships and one-square-mile sections; those in the Central Valley were identified with respect to the Mt. Diablo baseline and meridian. This system of rectangular land subdivision tied to the cardinal directions had been extended over much of the Central Valley—though not over adjacent mountainous terrain—as early as 1857.[8] Most towns and cities in the valley were also laid out in a grid pattern (although not necessarily according to the cardinal directions), so that the predominant geometry of both rural and urban places was no longer nature's gentle curves, but instead, regular and repetitive right angles. The speed with which the rectangular survey of many valley lands was accomplished reflected the desire of both state and citizens to promote the business of buying, selling, settling, and speculating in land. Although the grid had its advantages, it "contributed to a psychology that perceived land as a standardized commodity identifiable by simple plane geometry."[9] Maps with the grid of the rectangular survey, especially those that did not distinguish land by its other characteristics (such as elevation, slope, soil, or vegetation) contributed to that psychology.

An 1864 map by Amos Mathews of Yolo County displays the beginnings of irrigation in the Central Valley, as well as the pattern imposed by the U.S. Rectangular Land Survey (Plate 54). Mathews's map shows James Moore's small dam and irrigation ditch capturing water from Cache Creek west of Woodland. Moore's first dam was an easily washed out gravel-and-brush affair built in 1856, and his first ditch was just three-and-a-half miles long. Widened and lengthened in 1864, this ditch became California's only major irrigation canal at that time. It eventually irrigated nearly 15,000 acres of alfalfa and about 300 acres of grapevines. The map shows Moore in the simple act of watering his fields, but all his frustrated upstream neighbors and their fields are missing. The map contains no hint of the protracted legal maneuvering and hundreds of thousands of dollars it cost Moore to settle water rights issues with his neighbors.[10]

Much grander visions of a Central Valley hydraulic civilization were put forth in the California State Engineering Department's 1886 *Topographical and Irrigation Map of the San Joaquin Valley* (Plate 49 shows Sheet 3) or the *Existing and Proposed Major Water Developments in the State of California*, published in 1949 by the Irrigation Districts Association of California (Plate 62). The *Topographical and Irrigation Map of the San Joaquin Valley* was produced by California's first state engineer,

William Hammond Hall. The office of the state engineer was created and funded by the state legislature in 1878 in the face of California's myriad knotty water problems related to water rights, mining debris, flooding, drainage, and irrigation. Among the provisions of the legislation creating the new office were instructions "to locate and map all land capable of irrigation; divide this land into natural drainage districts; designate the best water sources in each district; determine the average annual water supply; prepare plans for irrigation works; and give his 'opinion and advice to such parties as may be engaged in irrigating a district, or who may be about to undertake the irrigation of a district.'"[11] The maps that resulted from these instructions displayed the immense possibilities for irrigated agriculture in the Central Valley and hinted at the long-distance transfers of water that might make it a reality.

Sheet 3 of the 1886 *Topographical and Irrigation Map of the San Joaquin Valley* depicts the area watered by the Kings and the Kaweah rivers. The map shows the extensive private systems of canals and ditches already in place, with irrigated agriculture extending for several miles around Fresno, Selma, and Hanford, and in a more checkered pattern around Visalia. A pattern of small (mostly twenty-acre) irrigated farm colonies had been established around Fresno. More striking than the map's area of "Lands Irrigated," however, is the area of "Lands Capable of Irrigation," a designation that covers about 70 percent of the valley portion of the map (with the remaining lands all located on the drier west side). Nearly all the map's extensive swamp and overflow lands—sold for one dollar an acre by the State of California even though in many places they were underwater only briefly each year—are all shown as irrigable. The means of accomplishing the irrigation of all this acreage are not clear on the map, although other maps produced by the State Engineering Department during this period include proposed major canals that would ship water into the San Joaquin Valley from the north.

The idea of a massive, integrated system such as the Central Valley Project took several more decades of population growth, the Progressive movement, drought and depression, and many more maps to mature into the first state water plan of 1931. Pictorial maps of California's water system, such as the one produced by the Irrigation Districts Association in 1949 (and reissued in updated editions until at least 1965) were used to display its heroic dams, radiating power lines, beckoning reservoirs, efficient canals, and grateful cities and farms. As the map itself states, it is not an engineer's map, but a diagrammatic effort "to capture the imagination of the citizen." The caricaturist's use of exaggeration is evident, with Shasta Dam towering over the Central

Valley and virtually all elements of the project enlarged so that the citizen "realizes their importance to his welfare whether he lives in the city or the country." Accompanying the map are tables of information that communicate the project ideal of comprehensive and coordinated planning. The map is a picture of the large-scale triumphs of man over nature, the smooth interconnections among the different components of the system, and the indebtedness of California, and especially the Central Valley, to modern engineering and science. The problems of hydrological conquest are, naturally, missing.

HISTORIAN DONALD PISANI CALLS THE DECADES from 1880 to 1920 "the horticultural small-farm

Pictorial maps of California's water system…were used to display its heroic dams, radiating power lines, beckoning reservoirs, efficient canals, and grateful cities and farms. As the map itself states, it is not an engineer's map, but a diagrammatic effort "to capture the imagination of the citizen."

phase" of California agriculture.[12] With transportation systems established, irrigation works under construction, and markets growing, land owners throughout the Central Valley subdivided their large holdings (*ranchos*, swamp lands, railroad lands, etc.) and offered them for sale. Four maps from Kern (1889), San Joaquin (1910), Fresno (1920), and Sacramento (1909) counties illustrate this activity. The rhetorical devices—both graphic and verbal—

Japanese-owned: Green; Japanese-leased: Red
Chinese-owned: Orange; Chinese-leased: Yellow
Hindu-owned: Blue; Hindu-leased: Purple

of these maps were employed to attract purchasers and settlers.

The Haggin map (Plate 56) is at the largest scale, identifying individual ten-, twenty-, and forty-acre parcels, as well as "town and villa lots" in Bakersfield.[13] An inset map, designed to show the location of the lands for sale within California, cuts off the upper one-third of the state, placing Bakersfield in the center of the map. The predominant features shown are the railroads, the farmer's vital link to markets. A second inset, showing the location of the lands for sale within the greater Bakersfield area, emphasizes the Kern River and the many canals already developed to bring water from it to nearby farms. The text that accompanies the map explains that all water rights issues have been settled (by the famous Lux v. Haggin case) and that buyers of Haggin lands will have access to all the water they need at low cost. The diversity of crops—temperate and subtropical—that can be grown is highlighted, as well as "the natural fertility of the soil" and the year-round nature of production. "Every crop cultivated by farmers in any part of the country will attain perfection here." Pictures of the New Southern Hotel and tree-lined Jewett Avenue promise an urbane Bakersfield, while views

of the Kern Island Canal and thriving peach trees testify to successful agricultural enterprise.

Themes of agricultural abundance and diversity characterize the maps from San Joaquin and Fresno counties as well. The San Joaquin County map in particular plays up the image of the Central Valley as cornucopia (Plate 60). It shows where alfalfa, almonds, asparagus, apples, barley, beans, berries, cherries, chickens, corn, dairying, figs, grapes, grazing, hay, hemp, lemons, melons, oats, olives, onions, oranges, peaches, pears, plums, potatoes, walnuts, and wheat are found in the county. The storybook style of the trees, crops, animals, and farmhouses communicates a cozy sense of prosperity and comfort. The text accompanying the map emphasizes how transportation improvements—road, rail, and river—make "San Joaquin County the Gateway to Prosperity for You." Classical allusions, both visual and textual, hint at a vision of future greatness like that achieved by the Mediterranean civilizations of the past.

The map from Fresno (Plate 61), takes a slightly different approach to selling its county. Mountains enclose and dominate the county, and the photographic images encircling the map show diversified agriculture as well as outstanding natural beauty. In Fresno County you get both "nature's garden masterpiece" and "the grandeur of a sentinel peak," both the valley's cultivated flowers and the moun-

tains' wildflowers. It is clear that the valley portion of the county is the garden, brought to fruition through scientific farming and co-operative methods of marketing and distribution, while the mountains are "nature's beautiful garden wall." The valley, in short, is made for cultivation, while wilderness and scenic values attach to the mountains.

Despite fine rhetoric, many subdivisions, such as the Sacramento Valley Improvement Association's at Clay in southeastern Sacramento County, were failures. Two-acre parcels of Tokay grapes and ten-acre parcels of eucalyptus were sold (at $600 and $2,000 respectively) to hundreds of buyers who in a few years lost all their money.[14] The map for the townsite of Clay (Plate 57). where every purchaser of a rural parcel received a lot, shows a railroad town layout familiar to Midwestern inventors (the company sold its California properties from an office in St. Louis). But glamorous California crops and a popular small-town image could not save this subdivision and others like it from poor soil, lack of water, and too much competition up and down the Central Valley. Clay remained largely a dream on paper (Plates 58 and 59 [photographs]).

AMONG THE THOSE WHO RESPONDED TO THE availability of Central Valley lands were Japanese immigrants. They began arriving in California in significant numbers in the 1890s, replacing the

Chinese (banned from further immigration by the Exclusion Acts of 1882, 1892, and 1902) as farm laborers. At the beginning of the twentieth century, anti-Japanese sentiment mounted as increasing numbers of Japanese made the transition from laborers to farmers. In 1913, the California Legislature passed a law forbidding Japanese ownership of agricultural land and limiting leases to Japanese farmers to three years. Many Japanese circumvented the 1913 law by purchasing land in the names of their American-born children or through Japanese-American corporations. Japanese farmers came to dominate the production of numerous commodities, including "between 80 and 90 per cent of most of our vegetable and berry products."[15]

In 1919, concern about the Japanese dominance of certain agricultural sectors led the governor to request a special report from the State Board of Control on the subject. As part of their report, "California and the Oriental," the board commissioned a map "setting out in colors all of the holdings by Japanese, Chinese and Hindus throughout the entire state" (Plate 51). The map suggested that "these [Japanese] land holdings and land products are in well-defined locations within the state and not spread broadcast. The Japanese, with his strong social race instinct, acquires his piece of land and, within an incredibly short period of time, large adjoining holdings are occupied by people of his own race. The result is that in many portions of our state we have large colonies of Japanese, the population in many places even exceeding the white population."[16]

Three of the state's five clusters of "Oriental" colonization were in the Central Valley: the rice district of Glenn, Colusa, and Butte counties; the asparagus, berry, vegetable, fruit, and vineyard sections of San Joaquin, Sacramento, Solano, Yolo, Sutter, and Placer counties; and the vineyard and fruit districts of Fresno, Kings, and Tulare counties. The nearly half million acres operated by Japanese were "the very best lands in California."[17]

The map and the spatial concentration of "Oriental" (especially Japanese) rural settlement that it displayed became part of the argument in favor of a 1920 state law forbidding even the leasing of land by Japanese and in favor of a 1924 federal law banning further Japanese immigration. The map of "Oriental" farmland clearly revealed the multiethnic character of the Central Valley, but only in order to discourage select groups. No one was mapping the distribution of Portuguese or Italian farmers and complaining about their tendencies to cluster in particular districts, like virtually all other immigrant groups. The key difference was the assumption that, unlike other immigrant groups, "the Japanese and their children were, and would remain forever, alien and subversive ele-

ments embedded in the American body politic."[18] Because of that assumption, the Central Valley's promise of abundance and prosperity was withheld from some.

MAPS WITH ENOUGH VISUAL INTEREST AND historical importance to win a place in a museum exhibit or catalog are usually the work of powerful interests. The maps of the Central Valley collected here are mostly about these interests, private and public, gaining control of the land and then making it pay. The maps and their makers helped spread and reproduce in the valley a way of life that extracted tremendous wealth (for some) from the environment through the application of scientific knowledge and abundant capital. The extent and flatness of the Central Valley are among the physical attributes of the land that aided this venture, discouraging aesthetic appreciation and facilitating an extensive, efficient, and exploitative agriculture. Alternative agendas—such as the preservation of natural landscapes, flora, and fauna, or the promotion of the interests of relatively powerless groups—found little success until recently. Today, environmental restoration efforts are producing maps whose vision is not only of the Central Valley of the future, but also of the past. Those maps may play a role in countering the old story of human modification told here. Recognition of Native American sovereignty, overlooked from the beginning of European and American contact, can be found on maps today as casinos and related developments add to the mix of activities sharing Central Valley space. New maps will capture and promote these and other emerging visions of Central Valley land and life.

Robin Elisabeth Datel teaches geography at California State University, Sacramento. A frequent lecturer on historic preservation and the social geography of the Sacramento region, she is also the current President of the Association of Pacific Coast Geographers.

1. Robert H. Becker, *Designs on the Land: Diseños of California Ranchos and Their Makers* (San Francisco: The Book Club of San Francisco, 1969), n.p.

2. A. L. Kroeber, *The Patwin and Their Neighbors, University of California Publications in American Archaeology and Ethnology,* Vol. 29, 1930–1932 (Berkeley: University of California Press), 257–259; W. W. Robinson, *Land in California: The Story of Mission Lands, Ranchos, Squatters, Mining Claims, Railroad Grants, Land Scrip, Homesteads* (Berkeley: University of California Press, 1948), 11.

3. The average length of time elapsed between filing a petition with the United States Board of Land Commissioners and receiving a patent on *rancho* land was seventeen years. Robinson, *Land in California,* 106.

4. Becker, *Designs on the Land,* n.p.

5. William H. Goetzmann, *Army Exploration in the American West, 1803–1863* (Austin: Texas State Historical Association, 1991), 75.

6. Donald Jackson and Mary Lee Spence, eds., *The Expeditions of John Charles Frémont,* Vol. 1, *Travels from 1838 to 1844* (Urbana: University of Illinois Press, 1970), 611.

7. Goetzmann, *Army Exploration in the American West,* 104; Carl I. Wheat, *Mapping the Transmississippi West, 1540–1861,* Vol. 2, *From Lewis and Clark to Frémont, 1804–1845* (San Francisco: Institute of Historical Cartography, 1958), 199.

8. Surveyor General of the United States, Map of Public Surveys in California to accompany Report of Surveyor General, 1857.

9. Hildegard Binder Johnson, *Order Upon the Land* (New York: Oxford University Press, 1976), 20.

10. Donald J. Pisani, *From the Family Farm to Agribusiness: The Irrigation Crusade in California and the West, 1850–1931* (Berkeley: University of California Press, 1984), 120, 340–341;

Joann L. Larkey and Shipley Walters, *Yolo County, Land of Changing Patterns* (Northridge: Windsor Publications, 1987), 39–40.

11. Pisani, *From the Family Farm,* 166.

12. Ibid., xi.

13. The land offered for sale at this time amounted to only about 7,000 acres out of approximately 400,000 acres owned by Haggin & Carr in Kern County. Much of their vast holding was never subdivided; it became the still extant Kern County Land Company in 1890. Pisani, *From the Family Farm,* 244.

14. Brandenburger Collection, Sacramento Archives and Museum Collection Center.

15. State Board of Control of California, "California and the Oriental" (1920), 8.

16. Ibid.

17. Ibid., 8, 53.

18. Roger Daniels, *The Politics of Prejudice: The Anti-Japanese Movement in California and the Struggle for Japanese Exclusion,* University of California Publications in History, Vol. 71 (Gloucester, MA: Peter Smith, 1966), 89.

March 27, 1843—It is true; this valley is a paradise. Grass, flowers, trees; beautiful, clear rivers; thousands of deer, elk, wild horses, wonderful salmon....There are thousands of different kinds of ducks here; geese stand around as if tame. The Indians make pretty blankets of the feathers. One can kill a fat oxen without asking permission; all one has to do is to give the hide and tallow to the owner. All soil products thrive.—from the journal of Charles Preuss, cartographer with Frémont's expedition

PLATE 52: John C. Frémont, *Map of the Exploring Expedition to the Rocky Mountains in the Year 1842 and to Oregon and California in the Years 1843-44.* Lithograph (by E. Weber & Co., Baltimore, Md.), 52 ½ by 31 ½ in. California State Library.

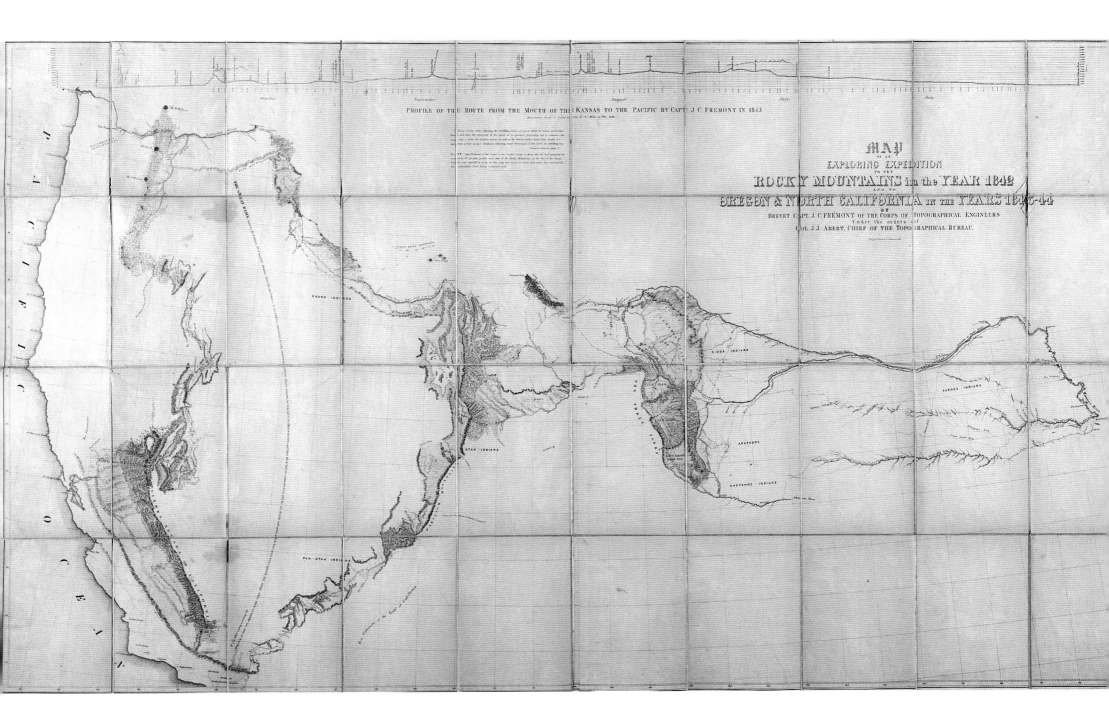

PROFILE OF THE ROUTE FROM THE MOUTH OF THE KANSAS TO THE PACIFIC BY CAPT. J. C. FREMONT IN 1843

MAP
OF AN
EXPLORING EXPEDITION
TO THE
ROCKY MOUNTAINS in the YEAR 1842
AND TO
OREGON & NORTH CALIFORNIA in the YEARS 1843-44
BY
BREVET CAPT. J. C. FREMONT OF THE CORPS OF TOPOGRAPHICAL ENGINEERS
Under the orders of
COL. J. J. ABERT, CHIEF OF THE TOPOGRAPHICAL BUREAU.

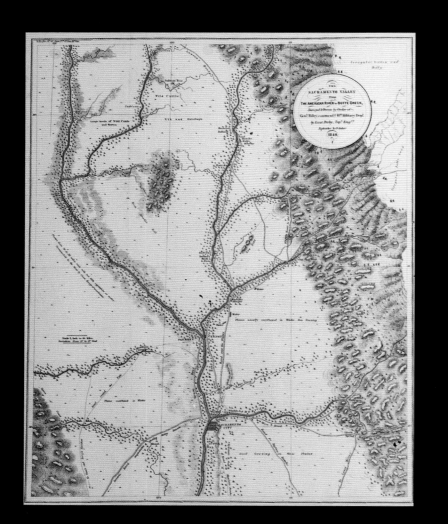

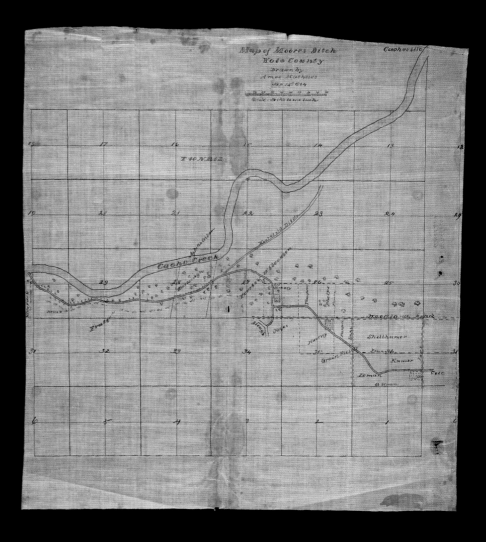

We had arrived within half a mile of "Puta" creek, when I observed with astonishment and alarm that a strong current was setting down the road, and that the water was deepening around us with rapidity. I at once comprehended that the creek had overflowed its banks, and that we were in a dangerous position. I gave the order to the teamster to turn about immediately, but it was too late—the mules sank at once on turning from the road, the wagon was fast blocked in the yielding mud, and the water, as we afterwards found, was gaining on us at the rate of four feet an hour. It was with the utmost exertion and no little danger that we succeeded in getting the mules extricated from the wagon, from which I had already saved my chronometer and best sextant, my drawing instruments and papers. We were compelled to abandon the wagon, with the remainder of the instruments and all our personal property, and return to Sacramento City.—topographical report of Lieutenant George H. Derby, Dec. 1, 1849

PLATE 53: Lieutenant George H. Derby, *The Sacramento Valley from The American River to Butte Creek*, 1849. Copy of the original hand-drawn map, 17 1/2 by 21 3/4 in. University of California/Shields Library.

PLATE 54: Amos Mathews, *Moore's Ditch, Yolo County, California, January 12, 1864*. Ink on linen, 16 1/2 by 18 1/2 in. California State Archives.

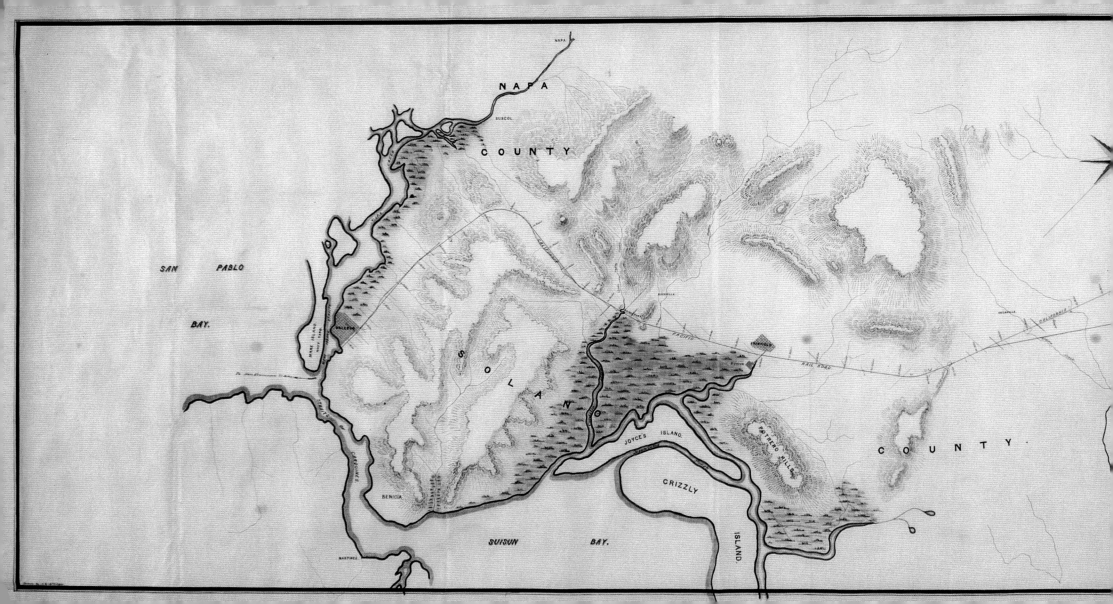

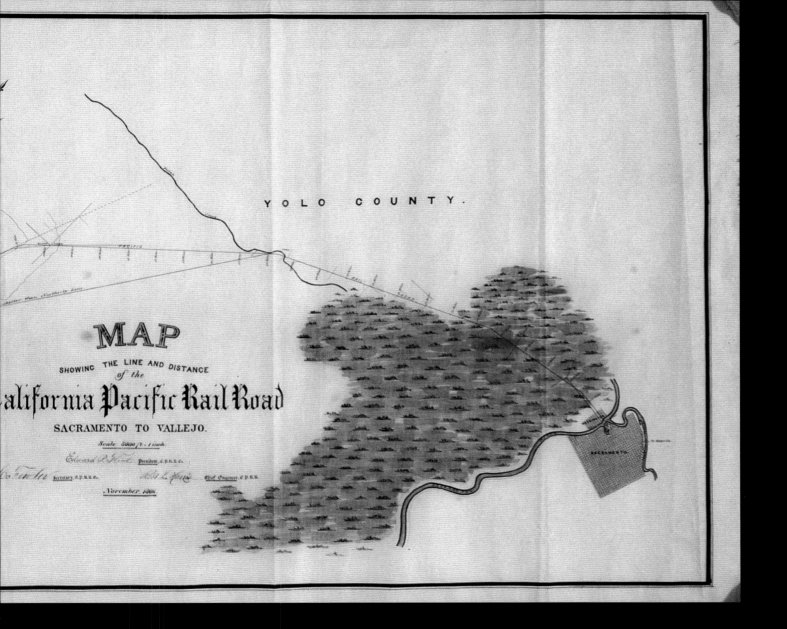

YOLO COUNTY.

MAP

SHOWING THE LINE AND DISTANCE
of the

alifornia Pacific Rail Road

SACRAMENTO TO VALLEJO.

Scale 5000 ft = 1 inch

Edward P. Flint   President C.P.R.R.C.

Secretary C.P.R.R.C.   Chief Engineer C.P.R.R.

November 1866.

This land will produce all of the crops of the temperate zone to perfection, grain of any kind, corn, potatoes, beets, pumpkins—
in a word, every crop cultivated by farmers in any part of the country will attain perfection here. In fruits, the peach, apricot,
nectarine, grape, prune, olive, etc., find here a perfect soil and climate. The orange, lemon, pomegranate, walnut, almond, pecan,
and other fruits of the subtropics also will grow side by side with those of the temperate zone. Even the banana grows luxuriantly,
though none has yet fruited here.—text from Map of Bakersfield and Vicinity

PLATE 56: *Map of Bakersfield and Vicinity, Showing Property of J. B. Haggin,* 1889. Lithograph, 20 by 20 ¾ in. California State Library.

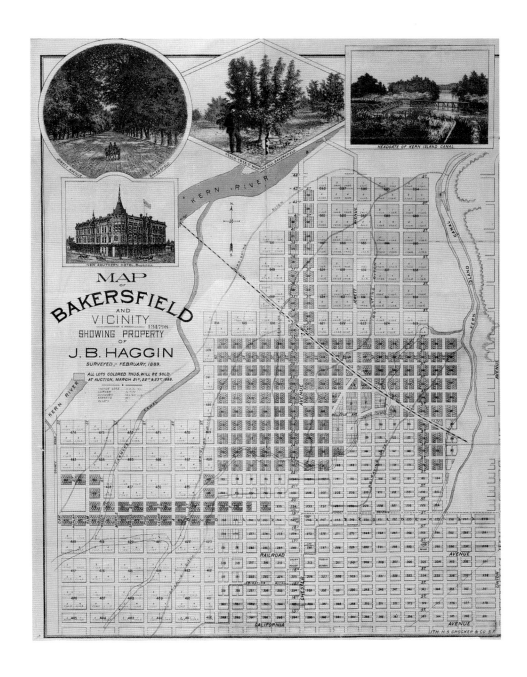

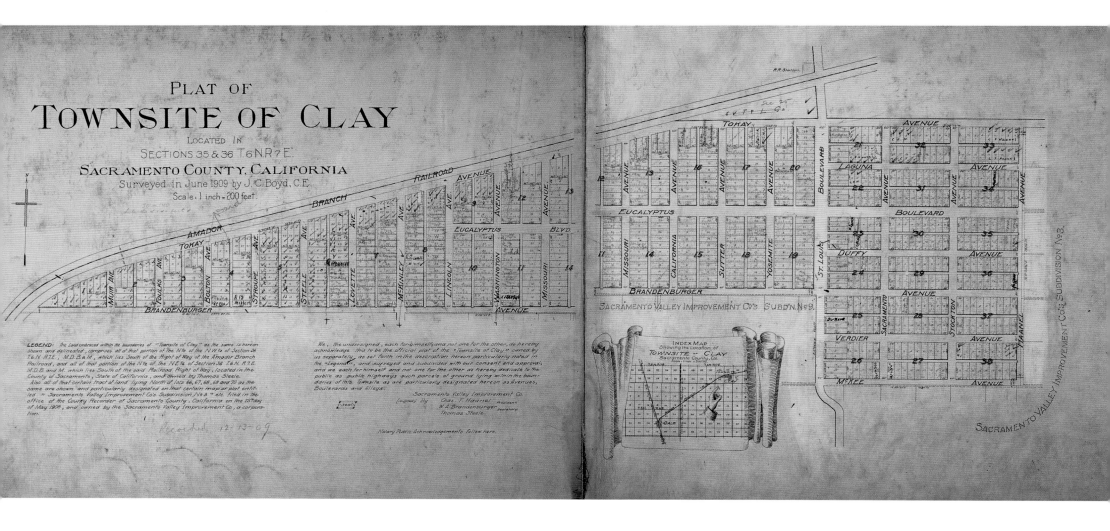

PLAT OF
TOWNSITE OF CLAY

LOCATED IN
SECTIONS 35 & 36 T.6 N. R.7 E.

SACRAMENTO COUNTY, CALIFORNIA

Surveyed in June 1909 by J. C. Boyd, C.E.

Scale: 1 inch = 200 feet.

PLATE 57: J.C. Boyd, C.E., *Official Plat of the Townsite of Clay, Sacramento, California*, June 1909. Lithograph with notations in ink and pencil, 21 ½ by 13 ½ in. Sacramento County Archives.

PLATE 58: Clay Townsite, *Looking Into Eucalyptus Grove*. Gelatin silver print, 8 by 10 in. Sacramento County Archives.

PLATE 59: Clay Townsite, *Looking North on Unimproved McKinley Blvd*. Gelatin silver print, 8 by 10 in. Sacramento County Archives.

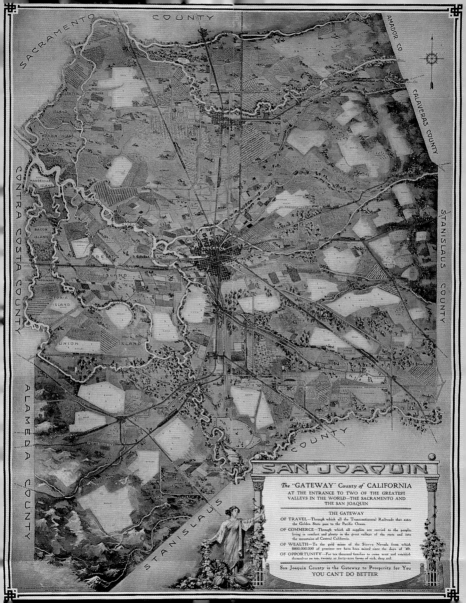

SAN JOAQUIN

The "GATEWAY" County of CALIFORNIA

AT THE ENTRANCE TO TWO OF THE GREATEST
VALLEYS IN THE WORLD—THE SACRAMENTO AND
THE SAN JOAQUIN

THE GATEWAY

OF TRAVEL—Through which all the Transcontinental Railroads that enter
the Golden State pass to the Pacific Ocean.

OF COMMERCE—Through which all supplies are carried to the people,
living in comfort and plenty in the great valleys of the state and into
the mountains of Central California.

OF WEALTH—To the gold mines of the Sierra Nevada from which
$800,000,000 of precious ore have been mined since the days of '49.

OF OPPORTUNITY—For ten thousand families to come west and establish
themselves on ten, twenty or forty-acre farms of rich, deep soil.

San Joaquin County is the Gateway to Prosperity for You
YOU CANT DO BETTER

PLATE 60: J. J. Rhea, *San Joaquin Pictorial Map*, 1910. Lithograph, 20 by 36 in. The Haggin Museum.

PLATE 61: Fresno County Chamber of Commerce, *Pictorial Map of Fresno County and Mid-California's Garden of the Sun*, 1920. Lithograph, 38 ³⁄₄ by 24 in. California State Library.

PLATE 62: Irrigation Districts Association of California, Water Economics Committee, *Existing and Proposed Major Water Developments in the State of California*, 1949. Lithograph, 36 ¹⁄₂ by 25 ¹⁄₄ in. California State Library.

PHOTOGRAPHS

"WHAT PHOTOGRAPHIC PROBLEMS HAS THE photographer faced and tried to solve?" This is the question I ask myself upon entering a new exhibit. Wandering around the halls of "Picturing California's Other Landscape," I see three main composition problems for photographers of California's Central Valley. Wherever they stand within the valley and whatever camera they use, they have to contend with horizon line, sky, and foreground.

The horizon line. It's flat. It's ubiquitous. It won't go away. You can move it to the top of the picture or move it to the bottom. You can leave it in the middle, which is about where it is if you level the camera and position the film plane perpendicular to the ground. Even if you hide the horizon line behind a thicket of brush or a suite of buildings, it's still there by implication. Although it stabilizes the view, it puts the viewer on what is perhaps too-even footing.

The sky. Most of the time in the Central Valley's Mediterranean climate, it's blank. It may be blue with sunlight, brown with smog, or gray with fog. Or white with non-descript clouds, the kind that imagination has trouble molding into familiar objects. Exceptions do occur in the fall and spring,

PLATE 63: Heath and Phoebe Schenker, *Picturing Yolo County,* 1996. Ecktacolor print. 11 by 14 in. Collection of the artists.

when major weather moves down from Alaska or up from Baja, California. But most of the time, the sky is empty.

The foreground. In too many pictures of the Central Valley, that is all it has: the ground, plowed and planted, or about to be plowed and planted. As a viewer, it is difficult to continuously look down furrows and over row upon row of crops without getting bored.

So what to do with flat horizons, vacant skies, and invariant foregrounds? During the last 150 years, photographers of the Central Valley have found several effective solutions. Living in a flat land, human beings put things up in the air. These structures break the horizon line, give content to the sky, and often make good framing devices. This is especially true when these structures are

emphasized by artifacts of camera and film. In *Yolo Causeway at Sunrise, October 8, 1998* (Plate 89) James Fogle divides the pure white, featureless sky into thirds with the bold, black, perfectly straight lines that divide his film into frames. Then, he allows the lone telephone pole to nearly unbalance the composition by placing it on the left, close enough to the frame line that its tilt is noticeable. This tilt is reinforced by the off-center ditch and the

David Robertson

corrugated iron, and partially offset by the road that curves to the right.

If a typical Central Valley scene of ground and sky doesn't come already composed, the photographer can always carry a frame along. "I don't remember where we got the idea," Heath Schenker said, speaking of *Picturing Yolo County* (Plate 63). "One Christmas, I think, out in the desert, Phoebe and I photographed a trailer through some sort of rectangle. We wanted to create a frame between artist and place to call attention to the fact that framing is a subjective act." So the Schenkers went to a local used furniture store and bought a 24 by 30 inch empty picture frame. In an empty field north of Davis, they hung the frame in front of the camera by duct-taping an old wooden stilt to an aluminum

A notable desire among photographers of the Central Valley is to introduce the dramatically vertical into the valley's horizontal world.

ladder and then suspending the frame from the stilt by means of fishing line. They picked a still day and avoided adding any "content" to the composition, like a farmhouse or stately oak. "We wanted to point out that things in the frame are different from things outside only because you've chosen to put them in or leave them out." The end result, of course, is that the Schenkers add content to an empty field and sky, even if the content is itself an empty frame.

A notable desire among photographers of the Central Valley is to introduce the dramatically vertical into the valley's horizontal world. Here, too, buildings come in handy. Roman Loranc, in *San Joaquin River Slaughterhouse* (Plate 87), moved his camera up close to a concrete wall and used a small aperture to keep both near and far in focus. Concrete takes up the entire right one-third of the composition. What look like splotches of paint and signs of weathering make the wall interesting in its own right. On the left, a low, horizontal wall permits a view of the distant, rather non-descript water and trees. An opening in the center allows the viewer to enter the picture.

Dorothea Lange quietly introduces the vertical in *A Very Blue Eagle, Tranquility Vicinity, Fresno County* (Plate 72). At first glance, all is horizontal in this image: the fence, the wings of the dead eagle, the horizon. But the bird's outspread wings hint at flight up and out of the frame, although we, the viewers, have to supply the flight in our imaginations. Also unstated in Lange's photograph is one of the major themes of Central Valley art: a loss, an absence of what was.

Photographers may use humans themselves, and not just objects they create, to solve problems in composition. Some of the time the humans are close up, with their accouterments, in and around their houses. Other times they are out working in the field—at least until the photographer arrives and asks them to pose. They gather around a work-related structure of some visual interest, usually in a setting where the camera can be held high enough, by hand or by tripod, to look down upon the scene and so give perspective. The photographer then distributes the human subjects throughout the scene with an eye to good composition and snaps the shutter. Carleton Watkins's *Artesian Well, Kern County* (Plate 64) is a good example. In this photograph, humans are small in a big land. Their shed, just off center, is used to break the horizon line. The well, surely the item of major interest to the landowner who commissioned the work, is placed in the foreground. The ditch drain makes a pattern through the otherwise featureless landscape.

AS I GO FROM WALL TO WALL OF "PICTURING California's Other Landscape," rarely do I turn my attention to matters of content. It is, in fact, rather surprising how little the content of Central Valley photographs is interesting in itself—unlike, for example, Yosemite, where Half Dome will hold its own in a mediocre print. Confirmation that content rarely holds the viewer's interest comes from flipping through photographs of farm equipment in the Special Collection Room of Shields Library at the University of California, Davis. Only occasionally, as

with G. W. Hendrey's lantern slides of the Schlichten Hemp Ranch south of Davis in 1919, does the content itself make the viewer pay attention.

But theme is another matter. Before walking out of "Picturing California's Other Landscape," I ask myself, *What do these photographs have to say, to me, to my peers, to my contemporaries, to humans everywhere?* One clear message is, *Humans are not at the top of the "value chain"* or, alternatively put, *What is of fundamental importance is product.* Frank Day Robinson's haunting photograph, *Planting, Merced County* (Plate 70), uses the horizon line and the blank sky to emphasize the insignificance of humans. Small and distant, people are stretched across the horizon in a parade of postures: stand-

Small and distant, people are stretched across the horizon in a parade of postures: standing, shovels in hand, bending, shoveling. A few telephone poles make a syncopated rhythm along the same line of sight.

ing, shovels in hand, bending, shoveling. A few telephone poles make a syncopated rhythm along the same line of sight. Extending from the field workers to the viewer are rows of plant protectors. The people are no bigger than the protectors, suggesting that they are one and the same.

What Robinson understates so poignantly, other photographers have put forth more boldly. In Robert Dawson's *Large Corporate Farm* (Plate 76), a single tree offsets the flat horizon and fills the empty sky, while serving as an effective protest against the procedures of agribusiness. In Gene Kennedy's *Tree and Displaced Buildings* (Plate 78), buildings shove the natural world to the side. His title is ironic: the buildings are displayed and, simultaneously, are in the process of displacing the tree. Richard Meisinger states the same theme in a more indirect manner; the two trees in his *New American Suburbs: Young Trees and Irrigation Lines* (Plate 79) are not the survivors of sprawl but its products. The bare ground around them is reminiscent of the plowed field in Dawson's photograph, but this time the bare ground is sown with a sprinkler system that will keep the trees alive in the valley's summer heat. Meisinger shows us what has become of *nature* in the valley. The view is not pretty, but the trees and pipe do make an interesting design.

Yet the notion that Central Valley humans are not at the top of the "value chain" has also been put forth in a positive way. In *Cache Creek Levee Line* (Plate 82), Stuart Allen takes a lone tree—in this case a deciduous *Quercus lobata,* the Central Valley's signature plant—and emphasizes its nest of branches by photographing it in winter. Then he introduces the human, not in the form of the sharp-edged plow or graded development, but as a figure of light making a soft, wavy line that curves gently in the distance and blends with other remote human lights. The image says in all but words, *The land is primary, but humans and their activities can make a visual harmony with it and its vegetable inhabitants.*

The message of Central Valley photography seems to go something like this: the land has little humanly meaningful order on its own. Humans must import an order, as the Schenkers carry with them an old picture frame. The contrast with images of Yosemite is striking. Viewers of those photographs are easily convinced that whatever order the print contains comes from nature, not from ideas in the mind of the photographer. With a nod to Wallace Stevens, an appropriate title for the photographic portion of "Picturing California's Other Landscape" might well be, "The Idea of Order in the Central Valley."

David Robertson is Professor of English at the University of California, Davis. A self-taught photographer, his work has been exhibited across the country. He is also the author of several books, including Photo and Word *(1997),* Real Matter *(1997), and* Yosemite As We Saw It: A Centennial Collection of Early Writings and Art *(1990).*

PLATE 64: Carleton Watkins, *Artesian Well, Kern County,* 1888. Gelatin silver print, 16 by 20 in. Library of Congress.

PLATES 65, 66: John Pitcher Spooner, stereographic views, ca. 1870s. 6 7/8 by 3 3/8 in. The Haggin Museum.

PLATE 67: Unknown Photographer, *Lake View Gusher*, 1910. Gelatin silver print, 21 ⅜ by 9 ¼ in. Kern County Museum.

PLATE 71: Chester Mullen, *Diver*, 1934. Gelatin silver print, 16 by 20 in. Shasta Historical Society.

I didn't know a mule from a tractor when I started. I got interested in the way in which [agriculture] was being mechanized. What I see now is that mechanization had brought about enormous problems…There is no place for people to go to live on the land any more, and they're living. That's a wild statement, isn't it? And yet, it begins to look as though it's true in our country. We have, in my lifetime, changed from rural to urban. In my lifetime, that little space, this tremendous thing has happened.—Dorothea Lange

PLATE 72: Dorothea Lange, *A Very Blue Eagle, Tranquility Vicinity, Fresno County,* 1936. Gelatin silver print, 16 by 20 in. Library of Congress.

I have returned from 1,000 miles of haze, smog, general dullness and three pictures of the Central Valley. Might be rich but it ain't attractive. I got turkeys, Lake Tahoe, rice and a squeaky fan belt.—Ansel Adams

PLATE 73: Ansel Adams, *Farm in the Rice Fields, Sacramento Valley,* 1966. Gelatin silver print, 10 3/8 by 12 7/8 in. California Museum of Photography, University of California, Riverside.

Flat land, open space, rising and setting sun, Sierras to the east, coastal range to the west…you can see the storms coming.
This was the Sacramento Valley. "Silver Ball," a container for rocket fuel, was slated for the scrap heap. A 1977 artifact from our
military-industrial-complex seems almost nostalgic in 1999, considering that these open fields are now paved with business parks
and their attending concrete and street lights. My daughter, "Number 68," has changed too.—Mary Swisher

PLATE 74: Mary Swisher, *Silver Ball,* 1978. Gelatin silver print, 16 by 20 in. Collection of the artist.

PLATE 75: John Pfahl, *Ranch Seco Nuclear Plant, Sacramento County California, June 1983*. Chromogenic development print, 13 ½ by 18 ½ in. San Francisco Museum of Modern Art.

PLATE 76: Robert Dawson, *Large Corporate Farm*, 1984. Gelatin silver print, 16 by 20 in. Collection of the artist.

PLATE 77: Stephen Johnson, *Kettleman Plain*, 1983. Gelatin silver print, 16 by 20 in. Collection of the artist.

PLATE 78: Gene Kennedy, *Tree and Displaced Buildings*, 1985. Gelatin silver print, 9 by 18 in. Collection of the artist.

The New American Suburbs: Edge Effects series is concerned with the changing character of the landscape created by the suburbs that are rapidly spreading around major urban centers, in this case the population growth between Sacramento and San Francisco. In the physical and mathematical sciences, equations defining relationships often break down at boundaries. I believe that similar failures occur in the disjunction between the social landscape of our suburban houses and the natural and industrial landscapes that press against them. Suburban landscapes that sprawl too quickly and without form create odd juxtapositions of shapes, open spaces, and physical incongruities.

I have much love for the unaltered landscape, and I respect the image of the landscape that is about to go under, or has just gone beneath, the blade of the bulldozer, for the sadness and sometimes anger it evokes. In my own work, I am trying to move beyond judgments about the appropriateness of manipulating the landscape. I take it for granted that man will eventually do so. But if the landscape must be touched, I hope that it is done with a sensitivity to aesthetics and culture and nature and the needs of the people who will now use the land. Photographically, I am interested in how well we succeed in this endeavor, and in the anticipated and unexpected visual consequences. There is beauty in that newly shaped landscape, and I am trying to capture it. That beauty is seldom classical; it arises instead from a real tension between elements of the image. I think that tension makes for a healthy relationship between the inhabitants of the landscape and the landscape itself.—Richard Meisinger

PLATE 79: Richard Meisinger, *New American Suburbs: Young Trees and Irrigation Lines*, 1992. Gelatin silver print, 9 1/2 by 19 in. Collection of the artist.

I photograph what I like. I like small-town parades and flag-waving patriotism. I like hokey. I like corny. I like unusual and bizarre. I like exotic, erotic, fringe lunatic, and everything counter-cultural. I like looking hard at our culture through all the various celebrations and gatherings we have invented for ourselves.

Photographers have much in common with people who buy metal detectors and spend their lives combing the beaches for hidden treasure. Probably they aren't going to find much more than bottle caps and soda cans and sometimes an occasional quarter. But maybe, just maybe, one day they're going home with a Rolex. It's what keeps us going.—David Best

PLATE 81: David Robertson, *The Eyes Have It #6*, 1998. Gelatin silver print, 16 by 20 in. Collection of the artist.

I have become interested in the relationship between movement and place. We experience a landscape's volume as we move within it—walking, swimming, crawling, biking, driving. The paths we make define our relationship to the land—trails, roads, contour lines, property lines. With this series of photographs I have attempted to translate brief acts of personal movement to film. Using a uniquely photographic device, the light trail created by a hand-held flashlight, I have introduced the simple element of line into these spaces within the Putah and Cache Creek Bioregion of California's Central Valley.

Photography demonstrates a remarkable ability to flatten space. These lines serve as a reminder of the third dimension. They were drawn in response to the topography and features of the landscape. The lines become a shadow of personal experience of place. In several cases, lines are created or reinterpreted by a force beyond my control. When things work out, the landscape itself plays a role in the creation of these photographs. It is this level of exchange that I find most rewarding.—Stuart Allen

PLATES 82–85: Stuart Allen (series of four), *Cache Creek Levee Line, Line Drawn by a Creek, Line Drawn by a Kite, Orchard Lines,* 1998. Gelatin silver prints, each 9 by 9 in. Collection of the artist.

I grew up in a mountainous region of Poland and spent many rapt hours exploring pristine trout streams and meadow marshlands before they were irrevocably altered by the damming and canalization that accompanied postwar Polish industrialization. Even though the Central Valley is a dramatically different landscape, my wanderings in remnants of the Central Valley's woodlands and wetlands are often, ironically, an effort to recover some of the purity and rapture of those early childhood experiences in my home region. The Valley Oak woodlands and freshwater marshes of California's interior, even in their fragmented and desecrated islands, invite patience and solicitude. Unlike the mountains or the coast, the valley is a "forgiving" landscape whose subtle textures of oak drape and tule mound, cottonwood glitter and willow blur, stroke the heart and evoke tenderness. At their best, Central Valley land and waterscapes are nature at its most eloquent: hieroglyph, thicket of the imagination and psyche, Thoreau's sanctum sanctorum, *as much within as without, as much sacred as hungry, always the dimension into which human beings reach for self-knowledge, wisdom, humility. The Central Valley I see is underappreciated and besieged, but beautiful nonetheless and still resilient and powerful enough to heal and to inspire healing.*—Roman Loranc

PLATE 86: Roman Loranc, *Living Room,* 1998. Gelatin silver print, 16 by 20 in. Collection of the artist.
PLATE 87: Roman Loranc, *San Joaquin River Slaughterhouse,* 1998. Gelatin silver print, 16 by 20 in. Collection of the artist.

This past year I have been working on a project about the sesquicentennial of the gold rush titled "Deeper Than Gold." What I have learned is that it was devastating to my people, to say the least...Today the mending of our society struggles with the continuing of tradition and appreciation of diversity. As we near the 2,000-year mark, it is hard to understand the changes that have happened to my people in the last 150 years. We should not forget the past, but we must forgive those who came before and move on.
—Dugan Aguilar

PLATE 88: Dugan Aguilar, *Two Worlds,* 1998. Gelatin silver print, 16 by 20 in. Collection of the artist.

Previous to 1987, I spent a lot of time driving through the Central Valley, stopping only for gas and food, a night in a motel at most. Without my notice, the valley was making an impression on me. This connection was revealed to me in August of that year. Landing in San Francisco, I hopped a bus to Los Angeles. The bus left at 10 p.m. and headed down Interstate 5. Around 2 a.m., the bus stopped for the driver's "lunch break." Stepping off the air-conditioned bus, into the night, was like jumping into a pool of hot tomato soup. The tomato harvest was on. To me, that smell and sensation were California, a welcome home I won't forget.
—James Fogle

PLATE 89: James Fogle, *Yolo Causeway at Sunrise, October 8, 1998*. Contact print, 5 1/2 by 14 in. Collection of the artist.

F.56 15sec 30m JiFog

Yolo Causeway @ Sunrise   10-8-98

$\frac{1}{x}$

COMMERCIAL AND PROMOTIONAL IMAGES

Residence of John Wohlfrom. *Yolo Co. Cal.*

By Andrew P. Hill. June 7th 1873.

DURING THE 1880S AND 1890S, THE SOUTHERN San Joaquin Valley was documented in numerous county histories and atlases. Representatives from companies such as Elliott (1883a; 1883b) and Thompson Atlas (1892) traveled the South Valley and found many settlers who were proud of their accomplishments and regional identities.[1] These townspeople, businessmen, and homesteaders were willing to pay to have themselves, their possessions, and their region written about and illustrated. As a result, the histories and artwork from this era are biased toward the landscapes and preferences of those who could afford to pay. Despite the selective content inherent in the lithographs, these works provide instructive testimonies to the events that fashioned the South Valley's landscapes throughout the latter half of the nineteenth century,[2] and reveal the attitudes, desires, and origins of the settlers themselves.

COUNTY ATLASES AND HISTORIES:
THEIR ORIGINS AND VISUAL ART

The public demand for lithographic reproductions featuring western images mushroomed during the latter half of the nineteenth century, owing to expanded interest in the region and the local

prosperity that stimulated self-promotion among the settlers.[3] Capitalizing on this trend, map-makers often included marginal portraits and depictions of property of citizens who were willing to pay for it; the subsequent compilation of this information within bound atlases and histories was motivated, in part, by the expanded opportunities for promotional sales. The shift to a book format was also assisted by the development of steam rotary presses and cheaper paper.[4]

Atlases and histories were usually produced on a subscription basis, whereby agents would initially canvass the county in an attempt to interest prominent and prosperous residents in the project. Each subscriber was required to buy the volume, then pay an extra fee to include a biography, portrait, or lithographic illustration of personal

property. In contrast to the comprehensive mapping and histories, the personal biographies, portraits, and visual landscapes seldom exhibited anything beyond what was directly contracted for. In this fashion, the landscape renditions within the bound histories and atlases were determined exclusively by the funding sources.

For the most part, the artists drew what existed, but the images they produced were not

William Preston

altogether candid pictures of reality. The view-makers "emphasized attractive features while softening or omitting altogether less pleasant elements."[5] They would often embellish their panoramas with people, carriages, animals, and trains to provide the impression of activity and movement. In the histories and atlases of the South Valley counties, trains, water features, trees, and foothills were frequently used, even though they were often nonexistent or lay beyond the line of sight. In some lithographs, anticipated developments, such as planned urban trains, buildings, and rural development schemes, were also included.[6]

The lithographs varied greatly in their quality and consistency. For example, certain elements in the landscape were often reproduced hurriedly

The most enduring themes that bind this set of lithographs are the expressions of permanency, prosperity, and commitment to place.

while other features—even within the same drawing—were rendered in loving and intricate detail. Perspective was often a problem for the artists. This is particularly noticeable in the reproductions of people, animals, and buildings that are too large in reference to items in the foreground and vice versa.[7] Nonetheless, despite their lack of distinction as great works of art, the county lithographs remain useful, albeit selective, documentaries of life in the valley during the 1880s and 1890s.

THE 1850S THROUGH THE 1870S:
THE FORMATIVE PERIOD

The itinerant sketch artists intercepted a unique period in the evolutionary geography of the South Valley during the 1880s and 1890s. During this time, the land was settled by large numbers of immigrants seeking to make this portion of the Central Valley their permanent home. This sense of rootedness and commitment imbues both the histories and visual art produced during these decades.

Rapid changes accompanied the Americanization of the Central Valley, and the processes that shaped and reshaped the region were reflective of those that eventually domesticated the entire western frontier. The gold rush had stimulated the repopulation of the San Joaquin Valley, which was virtually decimated of its native dwellers—the Yokuts—during the preceding Colonial period. By the middle of the 1850s, Americans were using most of the southern valley as a great ranch and pastureland in anticipation of the food demands from the gold fields and burgeoning urban centers. Without efficient transport, livestock proved the quickest way to make money during this volatile era. But during the 1860s, the South Valley pastures would gradually retreat in the face of environmental events and new economic opportunities afforded by transportation improvements. Severe flood and drought sequences destroyed incalculable animals and rangelands. As a result, a substantial portion of livestock-keepers departed the region.

This period also saw a strengthened transportation network of wagon roads and the arrival of the Southern Pacific railroad in the early 1870s. As was true elsewhere in the West, the presence of the railroad in the South Valley stimulated dramatic economic and demographic changes. With the advent of rail transportation, California's expanding cities, and the international demand for grains, an increasing number of residents and new immigrants to the South Valley began to pursue economic opportunities as farmers rather than as ranchers.[8] Beginning in the late 1860s and continuing through the early 1880s, the pastures of the South Valley were progressively transformed into wheat and barley lands. However, many of the grain men, like the stockmen before them, were not committed to the region as a permanent home, and a substantial portion of them sought only to make their fortunes quickly and leave. Not unexpectedly, their landscapes were often shoddy, transitory, and displayed few signs of domesticity.

During the 1870s the landscapes of the South Valley gradually changed as more intensified and diversified land use practices emerged. Irrigation was the key to the successful implementation of intensive farming, but early endeavors were initially hindered by both legal and technological restraints. An important hurdle was overcome by the passage of the Wright Act of 1887, which strengthened the access of cooperative irrigation districts to stream water. Moreover, greater access to water was complemented by new sources of power and technological inventions. Irrigation from wells benefited enormously during the 1870s from the development of steam drilling rigs and wind-driven pumps. By the 1880s, wind energy was being supplemented by steam and gas-powered engines that enabled farmers to pull water from aquifers under a greater variety of South Valley terrains.[9] Finally, the development of increasingly efficient farm machinery and refrigerated storage and rail cars allowed farmers to grow and ship to market a greater variety of produce. At last, South Valley inhabitants had acquired the power to gamble on farming as a profitable livelihood.

The new economic opportunities afforded by these developments coincided with the accelerated arrival of immigrants to the South Valley. Many of these newcomers prospered and chose to make permanent homes and raise families in the region; as it turned out, they also became the primary subjects of the sketch artists.[10]

LANDSCAPES OF COMMITMENT, PROSPERITY, AND DOMESTICITY

The most enduring themes that bind this set of lithographs are the expressions of permanency, prosperity, and commitment to place. Nearly every image reveals the external trappings of prosperous people working to secure a comfortable future in the valley. The ramshackle huts and untended ranch and farm dwellings from previous decades are virtually nonexistent in the pictured accounts of the 1880s and 1890s. Instead, these lithographs present the perspectives of people who had chosen to spend their lives in the valley or wished to entice others to do so.

Families commissioned a substantial portion of the country and urban settings shown in the lithographs. During earlier decades of the American period, men, mostly without women, occupied the South Valley. That began to change in the 1870s as women settled in the area as wives, homebuilders, and civic promoters.[11] By the 1880s and 1890s the female population was large enough to have a revolutionary impact on domestic and public landscapes, as well as on its male residents. Men, now raising families as well as working, needed more substantial homes; women, in addition to attending to necessary chores, were finding the time and resources to invest in the external beautification and public prestige of their homes and towns.

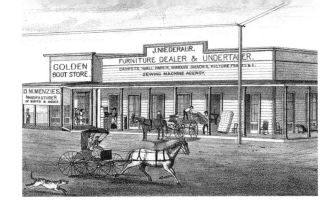

It seems that men were contributing to or, at the very least, complying with these endeavors.

The near ubiquitous presence of deciduous orchards and vineyards also indicate expanding opportunities and devotion to place.[12] These permanent plantings illustrate more than a simple agronomic choice; they became "an anchor that would enhance the attachment of settlers to their land."[13] In sharp contrast to the livestock and grain ranchers who preceded them, the planters of orchards and vineyards were intensely devoted to the welfare of their property. Permanent cropping demanded large investments and careful nurturing over a period of years rather than for a single season. What was done or not done today greatly determined the worth of the product during the upcoming years. In essence, orchards and vineyards were tangible expressions of the homesteader's commitment to a single place and desire, literally, to plant long-term roots.

Although only a small proportion of the South Valley farmers were able to make a living solely from their permanent plantings, nearly every ranch, farm, or rural homestead displayed in the lithographs possessed deciduous plantings of some kind.[14] Indeed, for the first time in the South Valley, even those settlers whose economic livelihood still consisted primarily of livestock or grain were becoming increasingly grounded in the region.

Their visual landscapes convey an interest in improving the worth and appearance of their holdings and providing comfortable futures for their families within the local setting.

Domesticity and permanence are also evident in the quality of the homes and business structures. Most of the lithographs of buildings in both the countryside and towns appear to be built to last. Whether modest or wealthy, the residences and downtowns seem to have been constructed of the best affordable materials and show contemporary stylistic flourishes in their Victorian designs, elaborate facades, and expensive wooden or iron fencing. These added touches rarely accompanied the landscapes that marked much of the South Valley during prior decades. Even the smallest edifice seems fastidious and illustrates concern for decorative pleasure and comfort. Likewise, commercial structures in towns are often imposing structures that evoke security, prestige, and grounded permanence. Money and care obviously were invested in their signage—an unmistakable indicator of prideful ownership and expectations of long-term prosperity. These images offer a distinct contrast with the slipshod structures and rough-and-tumble towns of most of the settlements in the 1850s and 1860s.[15]

Reinforcing this image are the frequent representations of ornamental plants. Many of the lithographs show efforts to beautify homes and workplaces. Decorative plantings garnish the out-door environments around the houses and feature prominently at the entrances to drives and door-ways. Even among the images of modest town dwellings, yards are shown embellished with vege-tation. These small changes did not go unnoticed. During a visit to the region north of Hanford, John Muir noted that "cheerless shanties" were "being displaced by true homes embowered in trees and lovingly bordered with flowers; and contentment, which in California is perhaps the very rarest of the virtues, is now beginning to take root."[16]

ALIEN SYSTEMS OF ORDER AND LANDSCAPE

The newly transplanted residents fashioned their settlements on designs and patterns that would have been familiar at the time in any well-occupied corner of the country. With only a few exceptions, the landscapes were shaped according to the background of their makers and reflect little in terms of the region's former physical or human heritage. The extent of this alien imposition is observable at every scale in these lithographs, from the regional layout of towns and fields to the plants chosen to adorn property boundaries and yards. Slight variations are noticeable, but the thematic diversity remains well within the parameters of the institutions, ideals, and materialism of the greater American realm.

During the early 1850s, American surveyors instituted a method of land division that became known as the American Public Land Survey System. This system was purposely designed to ignore the physical features of the land and to respect the relic property divisions fostered by colonial peoples prior to statehood. With the exception of portions of the northern valley, *ranchos* were sparse in the South Valley, and the surveyors encountered little resistance to their efforts to map and uniformly divide the land by means of celestial coordinates and perpendicular lines. Moreover, the pathways, boundaries, and habitats that had served the Native Californians for millennia were completely overlooked and were not considered in the survey. Thus, the first public land survey guaranteed that the landscape vestiges of the valley's native peoples would progressively and rapidly vanish into the geometry of American settlement processes.

During the 1850s and 1860s, the system barely emerged in the South Valley. In the decades that followed, however, economic and demographic changes helped to produce a type of settlement that would conform to this new geometry and provide its visual expression. By the 1880s and 1890s, most of the South Valley's inhabitants lived within town blocks or homes that were aligned perpendicularly to section boundaries in the coun-tryside. These dwellings and farms were also sur-rounded by drives, fields, and fences that adhered to the rectangular survey.

In truth, most of the central and western por-tions of the South Valley at this time didn't follow the national grid. These non-geometric settings are shown in pioneer ranches located on the outskirts of the more densely inhabited realms. Moreover, a few enduring relics of pre-American landscapes—including oak groves and creeks—survived even within the more heavily settled lands, and they contrast sharply with the otherwise orderly geo-metric scheme.

Interestingly, the most prominent exceptions to the Public Land Survey are actually human con-structions such as canals, roads, and railroads. Like the valley's streams and bayous, the settlers aligned their artificial canals according to the sub-tle, yet controlling, relief of the land. Routed with efficiency in mind, interregional wagon and stage roads were usually straight but were rarely congru-ent with the survey lines. Railroad infrastructures also deviated from the government survey pattern; the railroad magnates constructed routes and towns that optimized both transport efficiency and profitable settlement opportunities. The resulting landscapes were geometric with a slight twist: the tracks were necessarily linear but usually oblique to the cardinal directions; the towns had rectangular streets but their alignments were determined by the orientation of the tracks rather than by the surveyors' gridwork.

The geometric land survey was manifest over much of the American West, but exhibited most pervasively in the southern San Joaquin Valley of California. Here the land was nearly free of the territorial divisions of previous colonial occupiers and, by the 1880s, the remaining aboriginal inhabitants had long since been dispossessed of their ancestral property. With the exception of some lingering lake waters, the South Valley's unique physical geography was also conducive to the nearly universal cultural adherence to the Public Land Survey. Being relatively level and possessing few rocky outcrops, the valley's soils were composed of alluvial, lake, and terrace materials that were relatively easily worked.[17] As such, there were few physical impediments to bringing the cultural infrastructure into accordance with the survey.

The overall settlement arrangement in the South Valley did not evolve through a long period of intimate accommodation between the American settlers and the region's traditional cultural and environmental components. Instead, its basic organization imitated and reflected the web of parallels, meridians, and tracks that had been willed by the founding fathers and the wealthy empire builders who succeeded them.

ALIEN LANDSCAPE FABRIC

The illustrations of landscapes that punctuate the histories and atlases of the valley may have been very familiar to other Americans, but they would have proven alien to the eyes of the region's ancestral Yokuts. Indeed, very little in the lithographs is an outgrowth of a local relationship between people and the environment. Nearly everything shown had been introduced from afar and derived little from a relationship with the local setting.

That settlers imported their cultural inheritance is not surprising. However, the degree to which these foreign practices and materials were introduced to the South Valley is remarkable. American settlers were neither influenced by nor forced to adjust to a pre-existing cultural presence to any serious degree. In addition, the fertile land and mild climate were accommodating to a vast spectrum of imported plants, animals, and economic pursuits. Although local adaptations were necessary, adjustments to valley living were minimal, and basic American cultural traditions took root very successfully.

The domestic cultivars and animals represented in the lithographs are, without exception, natives of foreign lands. Indeed, even the ornamentals originated elsewhere, and the pastures were primarily composed of weeds of Eurasian origin.[18] Nearly the entire array of flora and fauna depicted in the lithographs was unrepresentative of the local geography.

Similarly, few of these buildings shown in the lithographs reveal new stylistic traditions that were an outgrowth of South Valley conditions or needs. Instead, the architecture closely mirrors the traditions that initially originated in northern Europe and, over time, were adapted to the American east and midwest.[19] The presence of the railroad insured that the settlers' architectural preferences could be satisfied with plans, building materials, contractors, and an abundance of affordable labor. Furthermore, the valley's environment was infinitely accepting of a wide range of imported construction designs.

MACHINES, RAILROADS, AND IRRIGATION

During and before the Middle Ages, it was common for European monks to decorate the margins of calendars with idyllic scenes of productive human endeavors. Likewise, the lithographs are accentuated with contemporary subjects and activities that record both the actual and the ideal. This brings life and movement to their sketches, and provides insights into the landscape and the common ideals of the period. Curiously, these pictorial embellishments rarely emphasize the natural or cultural heritage of the valley, but focus, instead, on the tangible determinants of successful conquest and settlement: railroads, power machinery, and irrigation.

The railroad was a major progenitor and lifeline to the valley's landscapes in the 1880s and 1890s, and it is prominently shown in the backdrops and foregrounds of numerous lithographic settings. By the late 1880s, the rail network had grown relatively dense, especially on the east side of the valley. Yet, it is doubtful whether every farmstead that was illustrated with nearby rails and trains actually had this visual proximity. It is also doubtful that the patrons and contractors for the depictions were disappointed by their inclusion. Much of their success depended on the railroad, and its lines were the most powerful representation of a modern and progressive civilization. Reminders of their accessibility to modern amenities and the reinforcement of one's linkage to the nation at large were probably welcomed by the pioneers of the South Valley.

Many of illustrations of the fields show men at work. However, the men are rarely depicted without machinery. Simple plows, hoes, and shovels are relatively scarce; instead, the lithographs show harvesting machines that are drawn by large teams of horses. Sometimes steam power is added to the scenario and prominently displayed. Machines, including water pumps, allowed farm owners to cultivate large sections of land efficiently and profitably. Evidence of the growing reliance on new forms of energy and powered devices were also reproduced in town settings. Among those illustrated are urban locomotives, industrial shops, windmills, and utility lines. The message is inescapable: the inhabitants of the valley possessed modern conveniences and would make nature yield to them using technology. These depictions of technology revealed the settlers' appreciation for convenience, modernism, and novelty.

Another common element featured in the South Valley lithographs is irrigation systems. In many of the vistas, canals thread across the landscape. Where nature was too dry for the preferred crop, settlers were prepared to reroute water rather than adjust to environmental limitations. Canals, pumps, and artesian wells provided the ability to

The message is inescapable: the inhabitants of the valley possessed modern conveniences and would make nature yield to them using technology.

pioneer drier lands to the west and farm the higher terraces between the river deltas to the east. Irrigation also gave the settlers security in a fluctuating climatic and economic setting. As one contemporary observer advised: "Be sure of water—whatever else you lack, see to it that you have this *sine qua non*. With it you can raise almost anything that grows on the face of the earth; without it crops will be uncertain and failure frequent."[20]

means, although not the guarantee, to win this gamble. In the context of the day, the generous and prideful display of these fixtures of modernity and economic viability is understandable.

HIDDEN AND UNREVEALED LANDSCAPES

The lithographs of the 1880s and 1890s present images of a maturing civilization in the South Valley. They display a remarkable remaking of the land—testimony to the courage, vitality, and arduous labor of the settlers. However, the lithographs are inadequate as profiles of the local land and community during this time. Absent are representations of the natural landscape and the unpropertied laborers who contributed so much to the drama and accomplishments documented in the regional histories and atlases.

From the perspective of the late twentieth century, the lack of attention to the biophysical features of the South Valley is curious. The region's soils, and especially the climate, were discussed at length in print. However, the visual art seldom places emphasis on the natural species of vegetation, native animals, natural hydrology, topographic features, or the environmental annoyances such as fog or mosquitoes. Vegetation singled out for visual attention is invariably a palm or unusually large fig tree. Missing are the remnants of huge oaks, cottonwoods, or even the

PLATE 94: *Thompson Atlas of Tulare County, 1892, Bank Building of J. Harrell, Visalia, Cal.* Lithograph. California State Library.

From the very beginning of American settlement, the land in the South Valley was used primarily for commercial pursuits. Produce from the soil was immediately integrated into American and global market infrastructures. As such, the settler had to gamble on fluctuating markets and cope with the unpredictable environment. The railroad, power machinery, and irrigation provided the tules. By the 1880s and 1890s, the majority of large animals—such as bear, deer, antelope, or elk—had been eliminated from most valley habitats; nevertheless, huge flocks of water fowl and a diverse inventory of bird and rodent life still filled the skies and populated the ground. Yet the landscapes chronicled by the sketches are nearly devoid of these forms of life.

Water appears in the lithographs mainly within the controlled confines of canals and wells. Streams, on the other hand, appear merely as secondary components, despite their importance in furnishing essential irrigation water. While the domestic plants that were nurtured by efficient husbandry and water control are shown in abundance, the negative consequences of landuse practices are entirely missing from the lithographs; in particular, these areas of the South Valley included the lands that were abandoned because of severe waterlogging, salinization, and soil exhaustion prior to and during this period.[21] Similarly, the topographic differences in the valley, although inherently subtle, are avoided. Attention to relief is present only to represent the proximity to the foothills and the Sierra Nevada.[22] Much like today, the South Valley is often more appreciated for its centrality and accessibility to the mountains and the coast than for its own physical attributes.

In retrospect, the paucity of attention to the natural ingredients of the land in the 1880s and 1890s is understandable. For the most part, these inherent features were challenges for the American settler. The competitors for the farmers' produce had to be vanquished, and any hindrances to efficient husbandry had to be removed. As such, the hogwallows and intermittent sloughs were leveled, trees were felled, and varmints such as squirrels, gophers, coyotes, and badgers were exterminated. Stream control and channelization were implemented, as well, in order to reduce flooding and optimize irrigation.

A PARTIAL DEMOGRAPHIC SETTING

A cultural profile derived solely from the lithographs of the period would also provide a very incomplete characterization of the region. The landless, the ethnically different, the hired farm and ranch hands, and the urban wage earners are all missing from these idealized representations. In particular, although the Chinese were well established in the South Valley by this time, and their domestic and service landscapes—the "Chinatowns"—were substantial, they were not portrayed by the sketch artists.[23] The shacks, tenements, skid rows, and make-shift living environments of the hired hands of other nationalities are also missing from the lithographs.

The absence of these humble people and settings is regrettable from today's perspective. Much of the subject matter was contracted for; therefore, the selection of images largely reflected the preferences of people with wealth enough to afford being documented in this fashion. This amounted not only to the under-representation of the Chinatowns and working class environments, but also to the assumption that wage-earners of any race were less suitable representatives of South Valley civilization.

When viewed from the vantage point of the setting itself, however, these residents are shown in nearly every depiction.[24] If it can be surmised that these reproductions honor those who built the railroads and canals, and worked the fields and tended the animals that so often appear in the lithographs, then the presence of the laborers is revealed throughout. Of particular noteworthiness are the Chinese, who served as the principal workers on railroad and canal construction, and worked the fields. Many Americans also worked as wage earners on the farms, in the railroad repair yards, in the building trades, and in the hotels. Without these people the landscapes in these lithographs would not have been possible. In this light, the lithographs of the 1880s and 1890s are the legitimate heritage of both the propertied and underclasses.

Despite the selective focus of the regional histories and atlases formulated during 1880s and 1890s, they are instructive windows on the life and land of the South Valley. Many cultural and physical aspects of that era were faithfully reproduced by the sketch artists. Through these images, we are reminded of the perceptions, success, origins, and dominance of the principal subjects and the people who chronicled them. Indeed, the civilization in the lithographs of the 1880s and 1890s is, as well, a metaphor for the prevailing contemporary values of South Valley civilization. Both the natural environment and working-class inhabitants are often overlooked as crucial components of modern prosperity. To a contemporary student of the South Valley, therefore, the ideals and preferences espoused in the lithographs of the 1880s and 1890s are remarkably similar to those that predominate today.

Commitment, domesticity, and permanence are the pervading themes that unify the South Valley lithographs of the 1880s and 1890s. These drawings capture the optimism, pride, and tenacity of the settlers who chose to make this new land their permanent home. Yet, unwittingly, the artists and their patrons captured the unrepresented subjects of their idyllic scenes. They also represented contemporary cultural presumptions and attitudes both in their choice of subjects and the domestic scenes that mirrored the more "cultivated" parts of the nation at large. These lithographs are a valuable documentary: they serve as a visual catalogue of the people, environment, and life of this newly occupied region, and they also reflect the more elusive actors and agents behind the scenes that brought these static pictures to life.

William Preston is Professor of Geography at California Polytechnic State University, San Luis Obispo, where he has taught for nearly twenty years. The author of Vanishing Landscapes: Land and Life in the Tulare Lake Basin *(1981), he has written extensively about environmental change in California.*

1. Wallace W. Elliott, *History of Tulare County, California, with Illustrations* (San Francisco: Wallace W. Elliott and Co., 1883a); Wallace W. Elliott, *History of Kern County, California,* with Illustrations (San Francisco: Wallace W. Elliott and Co., 1883b); Thomas H. Thompson, *Official Atlas Map of Tulare County* (Reprint, Visalia: Limited Editions of Visalia, Inc., 1973 [1892]). Many of the counties throughout the Great Central Valley of California contracted for similar atlases and histories during the same period; usually, the same firms and artists who had chronicled the South Valley were responsible for these volumes as well. The similarities in format, style, and content are striking for all the atlases and histories of the Central Valley, and indeed, throughout the nation. See Norman J. W. Thrower, "Cadastral Survey and County Atlases," *Journal of the British Cartographic Society* 9 (1) (1972): 47–48.

2. The South Valley in this essay is defined as the region of the San Joaquin Valley extending from the Kings River to the Tehachapi Mountains in the south. It generally refers to the valley portions of modern Tulare, Kings, and Kern counties.

3. See Ron Tyler, *Prints of the West* (Golden, CO: Fulcrum Publishing, 1994), 150.

4. It appears that these urban and regional mapping enterprises evolved directly into the county atlases and histories that became commonplace in California by the 1880s. For more information concerning the origins of county atlases, in particular, see Ristow, *American Maps and Mapmakers*, 403, and Norman J. W. Thrower, "The County Atlas of the United States," *Surveying and Mapping* 21 (1961): 367.

5. The railroads had founded a substantial number of valley towns and remained a powerful political and financial entity throughout the period addressed in this paper. It was in the interest of the railroad companies to encourage settlement and at the same time be depicted in a favorable fashion. This was especially true in the South Valley after the Mussel Slough

tragedy in 1880. See William L. Preston, *Vanishing Landscapes: Land and Life in the Tulare Lake Basin* (Berkeley: University of California Press, 1981), 131; *Reps, Views and Viewmakers of Urban America*, 70, 72.

6. For a good analysis of the content of county atlases see John Maass, *The Gingerbread Age: A View of Victorian America* (New York: Rinehart and Company, Inc., 1957), 188, and Ristow, *American Maps and Mapmakers*, 424.

7. Good criticisms of late nineteenth century commercial sketch artists are found in Ibid., 424, 463, and *Reps, Views and Viewmakers of Urban America*, 17–23.

8. Wheat and barley had been cultivated in the South Valley prior to the railroad's arrival and was shipped by wagon primarily to the north. However, the advent of rail transportation stimulated a rapid increase in the acreage devoted to the cultivation of these grains. See Preston, *Vanishing Landscapes*, 95. Despite these changes, however, the South Valley remained the last bastion of the stockmen in the Central Valley and farmers there remained handicapped for a time by the necessity of fencing out ranging livestock with expensive barriers. Finally, the passage of the "No Fence" law in 1874, which shifted the burden of fencing to the rancher, and the near simultaneous invention of barbed wire, insured a growing niche for farmers.

9. After 1884, rising land taxes and environmental problems (e.g., soil exhaustion and salinization) also contributed to a change from monoculture to diversified farming. See Preston, *Vanishing Landscapes*, 141–42, 162.

10. The relative newcomers who devoted themselves to intensive farming provided important subjects for the sketch artists, but they were not alone. Some of the extensive grain cultivators and livestock operators from earlier eras in the South Valley had adapted to the changing circumstances in the region, prospered, and were also prominently included in the lithographs.

11. Women increased proportionately in the South Valley from 30 percent of the non-Indian and non-Asian population in 1860, to 39 percent by 1880, and by 1900 they composed 41 percent of the population. U.S.D.C. Bureau of the Census, *Eighth Census*, 1864, 22–23; *Tenth Census*, 1883; *Twelfth Census*, 1901, 495 (Washington, D. C.: Government Printing Office).

12. Between 1860 and 1890 for instance, the reported value of orchard products in the South Valley increased approximately 93 percent. *Eighth Census*, 12; U.S.D.C. Bureau of the Census, *Eleventh Census*, 502 (Washington, D. C.: Government Printing Office). Also indicative of the rapid expansion of deciduous fruit cultivation was the 90 percent increase in production between 1890 and 1900. *Eleventh Census*, Vol. 5; U.S.D.C. Bureau of the Census, *Twelfth Census*, 1901, Vol. 6.

13. May Merrill Miller, *First the Blade* (New York: Alfred A. Knopf, 1938), 623.

14. During this period of increasingly diversified farming grain acreage actually expanded more rapidly. Grain production, for example, rose 98 percent in the South Valley between 1860 and 1890. *Eighth Census*, 11–12; *Eleventh Census*, 358. In terms of spatial coverage in this region grain reached a zenith in 1884 when more than 90 percent of the agricultural acreage was planted to wheat or barley. Osgood Hardy, "Agricultural Changes in California, 1860–1900," *American Historical Association, Pacific Coast Branch, Proceedings*, (1929): 221–22; *Tenth Census*, Vol. 3.

15. Preston, *Vanishing Landscapes*, 75, 87–88.

16. John Muir, "Letter From Grangeville," *Los Tulares Quarterly Bulletin of the Tulare County Historical Society* 80 (1971): 1874.

17. Botsford and Hammond, Real Estate Agents, Tulare County California: *A Truthful Description of its Climate, Soil, Towns, and Vast Agricultural and Other Resources* (Visalia, CA, 1885), 49; Preston, *Vanishing Landscapes*, 10–14.

18. William L. Preston, "Serpent in the Garden: Environmental Changes in Colonial California," in *Contested Eden: California Before the Gold Rush*, eds. Ramón A. Gutiérrez and Richard J. Orsi (Berkeley: University of California Press, 1997), 260–98, 273.

19. Harold Kirker, "California Architecture and Its Relation to Contemporary Trends in Europe and America," *California Historical Quarterly* 41 (4) (1972): 289.

20. Mary Cone, *Two Years in California* (Chicago: S. C. Griggs, 1876), 173.

21. Preston, *Vanishing Landscapes*, 134–35, 158, 160–61.

22. The emphasis on the mountains is particularly revealed in a drawing which is singularly devoted to showing the mountain peaks of the Sierra Nevada that can be identified from Hanford (presumably on a clear day). The peaks are even named for the viewer. See Elliott, *History of Tulare County*, 169.

23. The Chinese presence in the South Valley increased considerably in proportion to the overall ethnically Euro-American population. In 1860 the Chinese comprised just 3/10 of 1 percent of this population. By 1870 they amounted to 3 percent and had grown to 7 percent by 1890. However, due to forced exportations in the mid-1890s, the proportion dropped to 4 percent by 1900. *Eighth Census*, 22–23; U.S.D.C. Bureau of the Census, *Ninth Census*, 1874, 29; *Eleventh Census*, 404, 437; *Twelfth Census*, 738.

24. For an account of the role migrant laborers played and continue to play in fashioning the valley's landscapes see Don Mitchell, *The Lie of the Land: Migrant Workers and the California Landscape* (Minneapolis: University of Minnesota Press, 1996).

STOCKTON, CAL.

Published by ROSENBAUM & VAN ALLEN, Booksellers.

PLATE 95: Kuchel and Dresel, *Stockton*, 1856. Lithograph, 37$\frac{1}{2}$ by 31$\frac{1}{2}$ in. The Haggin Museum.

PLATE 96: *Palermo Colony*, November 15, 1888. Color lithograph, 24 by 36 in. California State Library.

Levi Painter lives twenty-four miles from Sacramento, and one mile from Courtland; he owns one hundred and twenty-three acres of land; was born in Indiana in 1833; in 1842 he moved, with his parents, to Missouri, where he lived until 1849; in that year he started for this coast, but stopped in Nebraska, and traded with the Indians until 1851; he then returned to Missouri, and engaged in farming; he worked in the mines there one year. He came to California in 1853; moved to Sacramento Valley a year later, and settled on the place where he is now living in 1855. He was married, in 1860, to Miss Mary McDermitt, a native of Scotland; she died in 1865, leaving him three children—one son and two daughters. He built, in 1877, what is known as "Painter's Hall," at a cost of $2,000; the first entertainment held in it was given during the holidays of 1877. His land and improvements are worth about $26,000.—text from Thompson and West, History of Sacramento County

PLATE 97: Thompson and West, *Ranch of Levi Painter,* ca. 1880. Color lithograph, 12 by 9 in. California State Library.

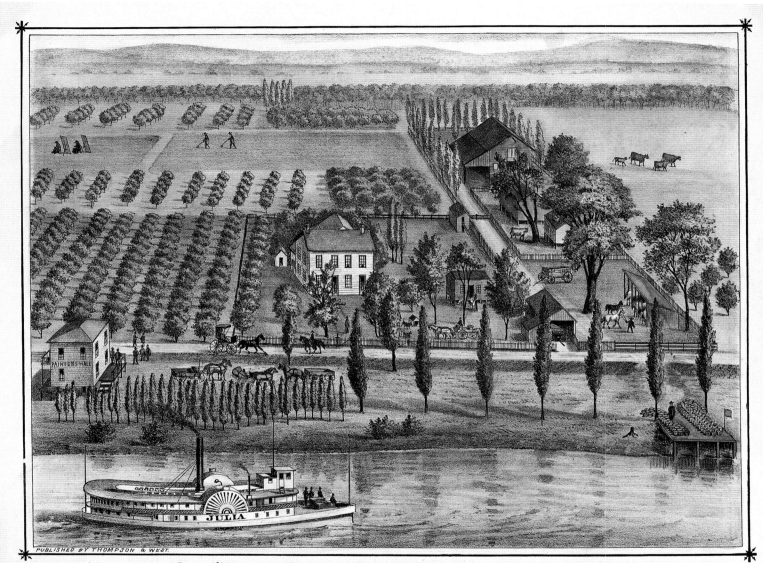

A VIEW ON THE FRUIT AND VEGETABLE RANCH OF **LEVI PAINTER,** 125 ACRES, ONE MILE SOUTH OF COURTLAND. SACRAMENTO C<u>o</u>,CAL.

BAKERSFIELD,
KERN COUNTY, CALIFORNIA.

PHOTOGRAPHS TAKEN BY ASHTON, PHOTOGRAPHER, BAKERSFIELD.

N.J. STONE CO., PUBLISHER, SAN FRANCISCO, CAL.

COPYRIGHTED BY N.J. STONE 1901.

Photo-Lith - BRITTON & REY, S.F.

174

PLATE 98: N. J. Stone and Company, *Bakersfield*, 1901. Hand-colored lithograph, 42 by 28 in. California State Library.

PLATE 99: *Thermalito, Home of the Orange and Olive*, n.d. Color lithograph, 27 by 40 in. California State Library.

Snowfalling is here the sport. Stockton Jan. 1 1916.—inscription on postcard back

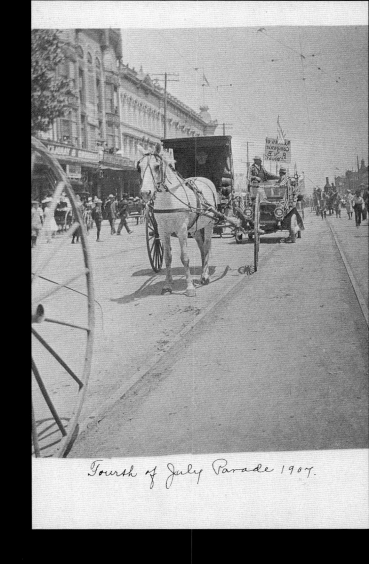

1907

Fourth of July Parade 1907.

PLATE 100: Postcard, 1916. The Haggin Museum.
PLATES 101, 102: Postcards, 1907. The Haggin Museum.

We are an explorer, a miner, an insurance agency, a farmer, a pipe company, a builder, a trucking firm, a gold mine, a logging company, a printer, an energy company. We are eighteen companies all across America waiting to serve you. We are also a railroad.
—a commercial for Southern Pacific Railroad

PLATE 103: Southern Pacific Railroad, *California: San Joaquin Valley,* 1908. Color lithograph, 6 $^1/_2$ by 4 $^7/_8$ in. California State Railroad Museum.
PLATE 104: Southern Pacific Railroad, *California: Sacramento Valley,* 1908. Color lithograph, 6 $^1/_2$ by 4 $^7/_8$ in. California State Railroad Museum.

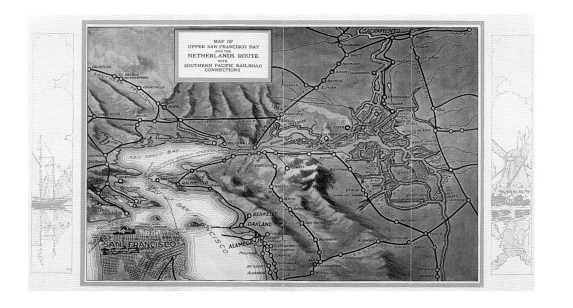

"The Netherlands of America" is a name that well fits the region contiguous to the Sacramento River, with its dykes or levees, the fertile lands behind them, the placid surface scows, schooners, steamers and launches busy in the commerce of the countryside.... From San Francisco, through the bay and up the Sacramento River—one hundred and twenty-five miles—this steamer journey to Sacramento, capital of California, is truly interesting and not sufficiently known. Traveling in a modern Sacramento River steamer—with its wide promenade decks, tastefully appointed saloons, cosy, spotless staterooms and excellent meal service—may not be as romantic, but is far more comfortable than trailing through Dutch waterways in a canal-boat. And sentiment, too, is not absent in our comparison, for the Sacramento River will ever be inseparable from the romantic history of '49.
—Netherlands Route, Sacramento River *Steamer Service brochure*

PLATE 105: Map of the Netherlands Route, 1912. Color lithograph, 8 1/2 by 15 1/4 in. California State Railroad Museum.
PLATE 106: Boroùgh, *Netherlands Route, Sacramento River,* 1911. Color lithograph, 18 by 32 in. California State Railroad Museum.

PLATES 107, 108: *Sunset Magazine* Homeseeker's Bureau, County Promotional Pamphlets, 1917. The Haggin Museum.

FRESNO COUNTY
CALIFORNIA

TWO SOURCES OF WEALTH: AN ORANGE GROVE AND DAIRY HERD

YOLO COUNTY
CALIFORNIA

Yolo County is the home of some of the world's greatest dairy cows. In the herd shown here are three record-breakers. In the foreground is Tilly Alcartra, with a year's milk production of 30,452.6 pounds

The city of Stockton, the natural gateway to the San Joaquin valley, is situated at the head of Stockton channel, a tributary of the San Joaquin River. About two miles to the southwest of the city itself flows the main stream....No other single element has contributed so saliently to Stockton's commercial eminence as the fact that, during her entire history, she has enjoyed unobstructed water transportation to and from salt, or tide, water, and thence to the markets of the Pacific Coast, the Orient and the islands of the Pacific Ocean.—C. D. Clark, Manager of Steamboat Transportation

PLATE 109: *Gateway Magazine*, ca. 1904. Color lithograph (cover), 9 7/8 by 6 5/8 in. The Haggin Museum.

THE HACK IN AN
UNACCUSTOMED
NEIGHBORHOOD

GENE THRELFALL
WM. MEYERS
MARTIN SCHNEIDER
GEORGE CUTTING
L. H. RODEBAUGH
MORT ADRIANCE

RESIDENTS NORTH OF NORTH ST.
BUILDING A SIDEWALK ON
COMMERCE STREET

The TWO BOARD
SIDEWALK
FURNISHED SPORT
AND AMUSEMENT
FOR THE BICYCLE
RIDERS

MORT ADRIANCE USED TO
SHED HIS RUBBERS AT
NORTH ST. AND HIDE
THEM IN THE CULVERT

STOCKTON'S NEW YEAR SURPRISE ON JANUARY 1, 1916 — FOUR INCHES OF SNOW

PLATES 113, 114: Crate labels. University of California, Davis/Shields Library, Special Collections.

PAINTERS, SCULPTORS

ROBERT ARNESON (1930–1992) was born in Benecia, California. He later moved to San Francisco and Davis, where he taught art at the University of California. In Davis, he lived on Alice Street, in the house that served as the model for *The Palace at 9 a.m.* His sculptures were often self-portraits or busts of friends and public figures, including a well-known 1981 sculpture of San Francisco mayor George Moscone. Page 50

ALBERT BIERSTADT (1830–1902) was a landscape painter, raised in the United States and educated in Dusseldorf, Germany. In 1857 he joined a surveying expedition to the Western frontier, introducing him to the vast natural scenes that characterized his paintings. Pages 14, 29

ALBERTUS BROWERE (1814–1887) was a largely self-taught painter whose first trip to California, in 1852, inspired landscape paintings and depictions of life in the gold mines. Browere returned to his native New York after a four year stay, but a second visit, between 1858 and 1861, sparked further paintings of California. Page 26

PAUL BUXMAN grew up in Reedley, California, and graduated from Wheaton College in Illinois in 1969. An award-winning artist, he is best known for his oil paintings and pastels of agriculture in the San Joaquin Valley. He currently lives with his family on a sixty-acre farm in the Kingsburg area. Page 77

ANNABELLE SIMON CAHN (1936–1996) received her M.A. and Ph.D. in Art History from Columbia University. A well-regarded lecturer on art history and art education, she joined the faculty of California State University, Bakersfield, in the late 1980s. She also chaired the California State Summer School for the Arts during its first year and served for several years as Chair of the Kern County Arts Council. Page 75

DALBERT CASTRO was born near the village of Holakcu—known today as Sky Ridge—in Auburn, California, and has lived most of his life on the Auburn Rancheria. The grandson of Nisenan Maidu chief Jim Dick, he is a self-taught painter who depicts his Native American heritage, tribal culture and history, and legendary tales in his work. Page 55

WILLIAM COULTER (1849–1936) was born in Ireland and came to California as a sailor in 1869. He worked as a newspaper illustrator until 1906, and between 1909 and 1920 he painted five mural panels for the San Francisco Merchant Exchange Building. Largely self-taught, Coulter drew upon his nautical experience in his precise depictions of sailing ships and rarely departed from the marine subjects that made him famous. Page 34

FRED DALKEY is a Sacramento native. He received both his B.A. and M.A. from California State University, Sacramento, where he has been a lecturer and instructor in the Art Department since 1969. His art has been featured in solo and group exhibitions throughout California, and he has received numerous awards for his work. Page 68

FRANK DAY (1902–1976) was born at Berry Creek in Butte County's rugged Feather River country. His father, Twoboe, passed along the Concow language, legends, customs, and tribal history to him throughout his childhood. It wasn't until 1960, after a crippling injury, that he began painting. His work reflects his intimate knowledge of the Maidu language, as well as the stories handed down to him through oral tradition. Page 51

DANIEL DESIGA is a graduate of the University of Washington, and has been showing, teaching, designing, and managing art since the mid-1970s. His murals, posters, graphics, and oils include reflections of the worker as well as the Hispanic and Native American cultures. His work has been exhibited at the Denver Art Museum, San Francisco

Museum of Modern Art, and Wight Art Gallery at the University of California, Los Angeles. He currently works out of his studio in Dayton, Washington, and is a part-time curator at Seattle's Galeria el Centro. Page 52

MAYNARD DIXON (1875–1946) was a California-born painter, illustrator, and muralist. He began as a magazine illustrator for various San Francisco publications, but he abandoned commercial art in 1912 in favor of murals and paintings with strong Western themes. For a time he was married to California photographer Dorothea Lange, and during the 1930s he painted murals for the WPA. Page 2

ROBERT ELSE grew up in Pennsylvania and received his B.S. and M.S. from Columbia University. In 1950, Else came to California State University, Sacramento, where he taught for over thirty years. He is now a faculty emeritus, and the university gallery bears his name. He has also exhibited his work in dozens of solo and group collections. Page 71

HARRY FONSECA attended both Sacramento City College and California State University, Sacramento. As an artist, however, he is largely self-taught. Throughout his work, he incorporates the ancient myths and symbols of his Native American heritage. A Sacramento native, he currently lives in Albuquerque, New Mexico. Page 84

DARRELL FORNEY was born in Portland, Oregon. In 1942 he moved to Sacramento, where he received a B.A. from California State University, Sacramento, and an M.F.A. from California College of Arts and Crafts. He began exhibiting his work in 1959 and joined the teaching faculty of Sacramento City College in 1969. He has had numerous solo shows and has focused on subjects that are "quintessential Sacramento" in painting, film, and song. Page 55

RALPH GOINGS is a native of Corning, California. He received his B.F.A. from Oakland's California College of Arts and Crafts and his M.F.A. from California State University, Sacramento. He has had solo exhibitions in Sacramento and New York, and his work has appeared in group exhibitions across the United States as well as internationally. Page 46

VIDA HACKMAN (1935–1999) was born and raised in Bakersfield, California, and her art draws on the historical events that have shaped the Bakersfield area. She completed both her B.A. and M.F.A. at the University of California, Santa Barbara. An award-winning artist, she also taught at various colleges and universities around the country. Pages 80–81

WILLIAM HAHN (1829–1887) was a German artist affiliated with the Dusseldorf school. In 1872 he came to San Francisco with fellow artist William Keith, and he remained in Northern California for ten years. His paintings are often large, detailed depictions of both city and country life in California. Pages 18, 28

HELEN MAYER HARRISON and NEWTON HARRISON are professors in the Department of Visual Arts at the University of California, San Diego. They are foremost among artists concerned with ecology, and their approach to ecological art often depicts vast expanses—such as entire river systems or large basins like the Central Valley. They have received a National Endowment for the Arts grant and international awards from Germany and Japan. Page 49

ESTER HERNANDEZ grew up in the Central Valley. A graduate of the University of California, Berkeley, she is best known for her pastels and prints portraying the political, social, ecological, and spiritual aspects of women's experiences. Her work is included in the permanent collections of the Smithsonian National Museum of American Art, San Francisco Museum of Modern Art, Mexican Museum in San Francisco and Chicago, and the Frida Kahlo Studio Museum in Mexico City.

For the past eleven years, she has taught at Creativity Explored of San Francisco, a visual art center for developmentally disabled adults. Page 73

ANDREW PUTNAM HILL (1853–1922) was a longtime resident of San Jose. He was both a painter and photographer, and frequently chose images of Santa Clara County as subjects. He was also a leader of the earliest efforts to preserve California's natural landscape, particularly the coastal redwoods. Page 28

WILLIAM SMITH JEWETT (1812–1873) was the first professional artist in California. A native of New York, he lived in California between 1849 and 1869, establishing studios in Sacramento and San Francisco. He painted numerous landscapes as well as a wealth of portraits, commissioned by Californians who were suddenly rich from the gold rush. Page 27

WILLIAM KEITH (1839–1911) first came to California in 1859. He began as an engraver, but his paintings of local landscapes financed his artistic studies in Dusseldorf between 1869 and 1871. Following his education, he spent the majority of his life in San Francisco and Berkeley. He often made journeys across the state with John Muir and John Burroughs, and in his day, was esteemed as the foremost artist of California landscapes. Page 32

GREGORY KONDOS is a longtime Sacramento resident, having lived there since age four. He studied at Sacramento City College and California State University, Sacramento, earning his M.A. in 1958. He later became an instructor at Sacramento City College, where in 1982, the art gallery was renamed for him. He also co-founded the Artists Cooperative Gallery with Wayne Thiebaud, Russell Solomon, Robert Else, and others. Page 57

FRANK LAPENA is a member of the Wintu-Nomtipom tribe of Northern California, and the places, events, ceremonies, and dances of the Wintu are central themes of his art. In 1971, LaPena began teaching at California State University, Sacramento, where he met Frank Day and became involved with the Maidu Dancers. His work has appeared in solo exhibitions throughout the West and as part of group exhibitions across the country. Page 61

CHEE CHIN S. CHEUNG LEE (1896–1949) was born in Hoy Ping, China. He arrived in San Francisco in 1914, and by 1918, after studying English for four years, he was enrolled in the California School of Fine Arts, where he was one of the school's first Chinese students. During the 1930s, his work was exhibited at the Oakland Art Museum, California Palace of the Legion of Honor, the Foundation of

Western Art, and the M. H. de Young Memorial Museum. Page 45

AUGUST MADRIGAL attended Columbia University for graduate studies in 1956, then taught for twenty-seven years at the University of Bridgeport in Connecticut. After his retirement in 1986, he moved back to his family's farm in Reedley, California, where he lives and has a studio. Page 78

ARTHUR FRANCIS MATHEWS (1860–1945) was raised in Oakland. He was the director of the San Francisco School of Design from 1890 to 1906, and also produced twelve murals depicting scenes of California history for the rotunda of the state capitol. He and his wife, Lucia Kleinhaus Mathews, developed and popularized the "California Decorative" style in painting and hand-crafted furniture, frames, and other objects. Pages 36–37

BARSE MILLER (1904–1973) was born in New York City and first studied art with his mother, Susan Barse Miller. After receiving formal training, he moved to Southern California in 1924 and taught at the Chouinard Art School. He also painted murals for the WPA and was very active in the local art scene up until 1940. During World War II, he was an artist-correspondent for *Life* magazine. He returned to New York after the war and taught at

Queens College, making occasional trips back to California. Page 44

JOSÉ MONTOYA was born in Escobosa, New Mexico. At the age of nine, his family moved to the San Joaquin Valley and became farmworkers. He attended California College of Arts and Crafts in Oakland, and later received his M.A. from California State University, Sacramento. He began teaching art at Wheatland High School, and did so until his retirement in 1996. A poet, painter, writer, and musician, Montoya is also a founding member of the Rebel Chicano Art Front (also known as the Royal Chicano Air Force), a group of writers and artists in Sacramento. Page 87

MALAQUIAS MONTOYA is both an artist and cultural activist committed to concerns rooted in the Chicano community. His work includes posters, which are undeniably political, as well as paintings, murals, and prints. Raised in the San Joaquin Valley in a family of farmworkers, Montoya received his B.A. from the University of California, Berkeley, and now teaches at the University of California, Davis. He currently lives in Elmira, California. Page 23

EUGEN NEUHAUS (1879–1963) was born in Barmen, Germany, and studied at the Royal Art School and the Berlin Royal Institute for Applied Arts. In 1904, he immigrated to San Francisco and lived briefly on the Monterey Peninsula, where he founded the Del Monte Art Gallery. He also taught at the San Francisco Institute of Art and headed the Art Department at the University of California, Berkeley, for forty years. Page 42

CHIURA OBATA (1885–1975) was born and educated in Japan. He immigrated to California in 1903 and began working as an illustrator for Japanese-language publications and on private commissions. In 1927, Obata traveled with Worth Ryder to Yosemite and had his first solo exhibition—featuring work from that trip—the following spring. Obata joined the faculty of the University of California, Berkeley, in the 1930s, but was interned at camps in San Francisco and Utah during World War II. After the war, Obata returned to Berkeley, where he taught until 1954. Page 38

OTIS OLDFIELD (1890–1969) used both watercolors and lithographs to depict scenes and subjects of California. He was born in Sacramento, but made his home in San Francisco, where he had his first solo show in 1925. In 1934, he became one of twenty-six artists to paint murals for the new Coit Tower. Page 43

ROLAND PETERSEN completed his M.A. at the University of California, Berkeley, in 1950. He continued his studies under Hans Hofmann, and shortly thereafter moved to Paris to study with Stanley William Hyter. In 1956, Petersen joined the Art Department at the University of California, Davis, where he played an important role in its development throughout the 1960s and 1970s. Page 58

RAPHAEL REICHERT received his B.A. from the University of California, San Diego, and his M.A. and Ph.D. from the University of California, Los Angeles. In 1971, he began teaching at California State University, Fresno, and has received numerous grants and awards for both his research and teaching. He was also the 1997 Yosemite Artist-in-Residence. Page 65

JULIAN WALBRIDGE RIX (1850–1903) was born in Vermont and came to San Francisco with his family at age four. Largely self-taught, he was a prolific member of San Francisco's artistic community in the 1870s and 1880s. Pages 30–31

MILLARD SHEETS (1907–1989) grew up in Pomona, and his work is often identified with scenes of that region. He was an art professor at Scripps College between 1932 and 1954, and he directed the Otis Art Institute from 1953 to 1959. In addition to

painting landscapes, he also worked as an architectural designer and muralist. Page 41

WAYNE THIEBAUD is known for his paintings of San Francisco's hills, with their characteristically bright colors and exaggerated perspectives. Born in Arizona, he was educated at California State University, Sacramento, where he later became an instructor. He joined the faculty of the University of California, Davis, in 1960. His paintings are in major museums and private collections throughout the world. Page 89

MICHAEL TOMPKINS received his B.A. and M.F.A. from the University of California, Davis, and subsequently taught at various colleges and universities. He has received two Individual Artist fellowships from the National Endowment for the Arts and has shown his work in solo and group exhibitions across the state. A Pennsylvania native, he currently lives in Berkeley. Cover, Pages 66–67

ELLEN VAN FLEET lives in Sacramento. She has traveled to various rock art sites in North Africa, France, Mexico, and California researching petroglyphs and Paleolithic art forms. She has also had exhibitions throughout the country and has been awarded grants from the California Arts Council and the National Endowment for the Arts. Page 62

THADDEUS WELCH (1884–1919) crossed the plains from Indiana to Portland, Oregon, with his family when he was just three years old. He came to San Francisco in 1866, where he worked as a typesetter and studied art, then went on to Munich, where he studied at the Royal Academy. He returned to the United States in 1881 and eventually moved back to the San Francisco Bay Area, where he began painting the landscape scenes that made him famous. Page 35

WILLIAM WILEY received his M.F.A. from the San Francisco Art Institute in 1962. Since 1971, his paintings and watercolors have appeared in both solo and group exhibitions across the country as well as internationally, including shows at the Museum of Modern Art in New York and San Francisco, the Whitney Museum of American Art, the Art Institute of Chicago, and the Museum of Contemporary Art in Los Angeles. Page 47

RALPH YARDLEY (1878–1961) was born and raised in Stockton, California. His first job was as a quick-sketch artist for the *San Francisco Examiner;* he later worked as an artist for the *Honolulu Advertiser, New York Globe,* and *San Francisco Call.* In 1921, he returned to Stockton, where he enjoyed a thirty-year career as a cartoonist for the *Stockton Record.* Pages 186–187

RAYMOND DABB YELLAND (1848–1900) came to California in 1873 to teach at Mills College in Oakland. He later became an instructor at the San Francisco School of Design, and eventually became its director in 1888. His collection of landscape paintings depict the coastlines and natural landscapes of California. Page 33

HIDEO CHESTER YOSHIDA lives in San Francisco. He attended both the San Francisco Art Institute and the Art Center College of Design in Los Angeles. He has taught printmaking, design, fashion drawing, and silk-screen at various institutions in San Francisco. An award-winning set designer, he has also received fellowships from *Mother Jones* magazine and the San Francisco Art Commission. Page 83

PHOTOGRAPHERS

ANSEL ADAMS (1902–1984) was born in San Francisco and is world-renowned for his photographs of Yosemite and a vast array of other wilderness scenes. He was also actively involved in efforts to preserve California's natural landscape. His photographs have been widely exhibited in prominent museums, and roughly thirty books on his photography have been published. Page 132

DUGAN AGUILAR is of Paiute/Pit River/Maidu heritage, and his work celebrates the perseverance of Native American culture. Born in Susanville, California, he graduated from California State University, Fresno, and attended the University of Nevada, Reno. He has exhibited his work at the Institute for Indian Arts, the California State Indian Museum, and the C. N. Gorman Museum, and his photographs will be featured in *Deeper Than Gold: Indian Life Along California's Highway 49* (1999). He lives in Elk Grove, California. Page 152

STUART ALLEN was born in Wichita, Kansas. He received a degree from the Kansas City Art Institute in 1993 and has received numerous awards, grants, and commissions for his work, including a Public Art Commission for a permanent installation at the United States Embassy in Ottawa, Canada. Pages 148–149

DAVID BEST discovered his passion for photography at age eight, when he bought an Ansel Adams poster of Lone Pine for his bedroom wall. Much of his training came from working with Gene Kennedy at The Darkroom in Sacramento. He now lives in Lodi, California, where he photographs unusual events and renovates old houses. Pages 144–145

ROBERT DAWSON is a native of the Central Valley. He received a B.A. from the University of California, Santa Cruz, and an M.A. from San Francisco State University. His award-winning work has appeared in numerous exhibitions and publications, including *Robert Dawson Photographs* (1998). With Stephen Johnson, he also created the exhibits "The Great Central Valley Project" and "The Great Central Valley: California's Heartland." He currently teaches at both San Jose State University and City College of San Francisco. Page 137

JAMES FOGLE grew up in Burbank, California, and graduated from California State University, Long Beach, with a B.S. in physical therapy. He is a self-taught photographer whose work has been shown at the Davis Art Center and the Camera Arts group show. He is also the 1998/1999 recipient of the Putah Cache Bioregion Project Artist-in-Residence Award. Page 155

STEPHEN JOHNSON was born in Merced, California, and earned his B.A. and M.A. from San Francisco State University. He edited and designed his first book, *At Mono Lake* (1983), for which he received a grant from the National Endowment for the Arts. With Robert Dawson, he also created the exhibits "The Great Central Valley Project" and "The Great Central Valley: California's Heartland." He currently teaches photography at Foothill College in Los Altos Hills and has run his own photography workshop since 1977. Page 139

GENE KENNEDY was born in San Diego and moved to the Sacramento Valley in 1985. After receiving his B.A. and M.A. in Industrial Arts from San Diego State University, he taught at various colleges and universities throughout the state. He has received a number of awards and grants and has published monographs, articles, and a textbook, *A Sourcebook for Intermediate Photography*. He is also the managing editor of *View Camera* and *Camera Arts* magazines. Pages 140–141

DOROTHEA LANGE (1895–1965) was a New Jersey-born photographer. She moved to California in 1918 and established a studio in San Francisco, where she married the artist Maynard Dixon. In 1940 her pictures of the bleak experience of migrant farm laborers during the Depression were

published in *American Exodus.* Her later work remained socially conscious and included photographs of the Japanese internment camps during World War II. Page 131

ROMAN LORANC was born in Bielsko-Biala, Poland, and emigrated to the United States in 1981. In 1984 he moved to California, where he rekindled his childhood interest in landscape photography and eventually settled in the Central Valley. He has had solo exhibitions in California and Poland, and his work was featured in *Highway 99: A Literary Journey Through California's Great Central Valley.* He and his wife, writer Lillian Vallee, are currently collaborating on a book entitled *Hardworking Rivers: The Streams and Wetlands of the San Joaquin Valley.* Page 151

RICHARD MEISINGER received his Ph.D. from the University of California, Berkeley. His work has been featured in various California exhibitions over the last ten years, including two shows on the Central Valley. He has won several awards for his work, and his photographs have been published in books and magazines. He is currently Associate Provost at the University of California, Davis. Page 143

CHESTER MULLEN (1886–1958) was born in Redding, California, to the son of Irish immigrants who had settled in the upper portion of the Central Valley when it was nothing more than a manzanita-covered terrace called Poverty Flat. A carpenter by trade, Mullen was first hired as a photographer by local insurance companies to photograph damaged autos, then by the city to take mug shots of jail inmates. He lived in Redding until 1939, then moved with his wife to Shasta. After his death in 1958, his equipment and negatives were given to the Shasta Historical Society, who restored the damaged negatives. Page 128

JOHN PFAHL grew up in New Jersey and received an M.A. from Syracuse University; immediately afterward, he joined the faculty of Rochester Institute of Technology. He traveled regularly to California to meet with Ansel Adams, to lecture at workshops, and to photograph the landscape. He has received a grant from the National Endowment for the Arts, as well as the New York State Creative Artists Public Service Grant. Page 136

DAVID ROBERTSON received his B.A. from Yale, his B.D. from Perkins School of Theology, his M.S. from the University of Toronto, and Ph.D.s from both Yale and the University of California, Irvine. Born in Memphis, Tennessee, he is a self-taught photographer. He was twice a Yosemite Artist-in-

Residence and has published a number of books, including *West of Eden* (1984), *Yosemite As We Saw It* (1990), and *Real Matter* (1997). Currently, he is Professor of English at the University of California, Davis, and a founding member of the Putah Cache Bioregion Project. Page 147

FRANK DAY ROBINSON was nearly an undiscovered talent. His glass-plate negatives were discovered and retrieved from the Merced County Dump sometime in the 1940s. They sat in a local garage for forty more years until James Docherty started to print and preserve the collection. Robinson's work, circa 1925, also appears in *The Great Central Valley: California's Heartland.* Page 127

HEATH SCHENKER is a landscape architect and recipient of merit awards from the American Society of Landscape Architects and the California Council of Landscape Architects. Her work has been exhibited around the country and published in various books and design journals. Page 116

PHOEBE SCHENKER is an architecture student at the University of California, Berkeley, and recently spent a year studying architecture in Cambridge, England. She was a California Arts Scholar in 1996, attending the California State Summer School of the Arts at Cal Arts, Valencia. Page 116

JOHN PITCHER SPOONER (1845–1917) was a native of Massachusetts. He opened a photography studio in Stockton in the early 1870s, and for more than forty years he captured images of the area and its residents. Today, his work forms one of the largest and most historically significant photographic records of San Joaquin County. Pages 122-123

MARY SWISHER has a B.A. in Fine Arts, an M.A. in Photography, and has done post-graduate study in painting. She received two National Endowment for the Arts grants as well as a California Arts Council award to research photography in the Sacramento Valley and to curate a traveling exhibition, "Commercial Photography of the Sacramento Valley." Her work has been shown in museums throughout the world, and she has had two solo exhibits at the Crocker Art Museum in Sacramento. Page 135

CARLETON WATKINS (1829–1916) moved to California during the gold rush and rapidly became one of the state's most prominent photographers. His vast landscape pictures captured scenes of Yosemite, the crumbling California missions, and other images that illustrated life in the West during the second half of the nineteenth century. Page 121

PERMISSIONS

PLATE 1: Maynard Dixon, *Approaching Storm.* Courtesy of the Fresno Metropolitan Museum. PLATE 2: unknown, Crate Label. Courtesy of the Shields Library, University of California, Davis. Special Collections. PLATE 3: Raven Map of California. © 1987 Raven Maps & Images. Photo by Greg Kinder. PLATE 4: Albert Bierstadt, *California Spring.* Courtesy of the Fine Arts Museums of San Francisco. Presented to the City and County of San Francisco by Gordon Blanding. PLATE 5: William Hahn, *Harvest Time.* Courtesy of The Fine Arts Museums of San Francisco, Gift of Mrs. Harold R. McKinnon and Mrs. Harry L. Brown. PLATE 6: Malaquias Montoya, *Come Siempre Raza.* Courtesy of the artist. PLATE 7: Albertus Browere, *A View of Stockton.* Courtesy of The Haggin Museum, Stockton, California. PLATE 8: William Smith Jewett, *Hock Farm.* Courtesy of the State of California, California State Parks Resource Center, West Sacramento, California. PLATE 9: William Hahn, *Sacramento Railroad Station.* Courtesy of Fine Arts Museums of San Francisco. Gift of the M. H. de Young Endowment Fund. PLATE 10: Andrew Putnam Hill, *Jacinto Ranch Harvest Scene.* Courtesy of The Haggin Museum, Stockton, California. Gift of Mr. and Mrs. Joseph Parker. PLATE 11: Albert Bierstadt, *Forest Monarchs.* Courtesy of The Haggin Museum, Stockton, California. The Haggin Collection. PLATE 12: Julian Walbridge Rix, *Upper Sacramento River.* Courtesy of the Garzoli Gallery, San Rafael, California. PLATE 13: William Keith, *Sunset Near Suisun.* Courtesy of the Oakland Museum of California. The Wall Collection. PLATE 14: Raymond Dabb Yelland, *Sunrise at Tracy.* Courtesy of the Oakland Museum of California. Gift of Mr. and Mrs. William B. Land. PLATE 15: William Coulter, *Stockton Channel.* Courtesy of The Haggin Museum, Stockton, California. Gift of Reed M. Clarke. PLATE 16: Thaddeus Welch, *Jewett Ranch.* Courtesy of the Kern County Museum. PLATE 17: Arthur Francis Mathews, *Sketches for the Capitol Rotunda: Epoch III* Courtesy of the California State Library. Photo by Greg Kinder. PLATE 18: Chiura Obata, *Sunset in the Sacramento Valley.* Courtesy of the Crocker Art Museum, Sacramento, California. Gift of the family of Chiura Obata. PLATE 19: Millard Sheets, *Walnut Creek Canyon.* Courtesy of Michael Johnson Fine Arts. PLATE 20: Eugen Neuhaus, *Sutter Buttes.* Courtesy of the Oakland Museum of California. Gift of Mr. and Mrs. Robert Neuhaus. PLATE 21: Otis Oldfield, *Steamboat Landing.* Courtesy of Jayne Blatchly. The Estate of Otis Oldfield and the Jayne Blatchly Trust. PLATE 22: Barse Miller, *Along the Sacramento.* Courtesy of the Crocker Art Museum, Sacramento, California. Gift of Mrs. Barse Miller. PLATE 23: Chee Chin S. Cheung Lee, *The Valley.* Courtesy of the Michael D. Brown Collection. PLATE 24: Ralph Goings, *Camper Truck.* Courtesy of the Crocker Art Museum, Sacramento, California. Gift of the Crocker Art Gallery Association. PLATE 25: William

Wiley, *Valley Fog Cutter.* Courtesy of the Richard L. Nelson Gallery and The Fine Arts Collection, University of California, Davis. PLATE 26: Helen Mayer Harrison and Newton Harrison, *Meditations on the Sacramento River, the Delta and the Bays of San Francisco.* Courtesy of the artists. PLATE 27: Robert Arneson, *The Palace at 9 a.m.* Courtesy of Brian Gross Fine Arts, San Francisco, California. PLATE 28: Frank Day, *Fish Dancer.* Courtesy of Leigh and Sandra Marymor. PLATE 29: Daniel DeSiga, *Campesino.* Courtesy of UCLA at the Armand Hammer Museum of Art and Cultural Center, Los Angeles. Collection of Alfredo Aragón. PLATE 30: Darrell Forney, *Archimedes Screw.* Courtesy of the artist. PLATE 31: Dalbert Castro, *Maidu Walk.* Courtesy of the Oakland Museum of California. PLATE 32: Gregory Kondos, *Sacramento River.* Courtesy of the Crocker Art Museum, Sacramento, California. Gift of the First Interstate Bank of California. PLATE 33: Roland Petersen, *Picnic with Four Figures.* Courtesy of the Richard L. Nelson Gallery and The Fine Arts Collection, University of California, Davis. PLATE 34: Frank LaPena, *Hesi Spirit.* Courtesy of the Natsoulas Gallery, Davis, California. Photo by Greg Kinder. PLATE 35: Ellen Van Fleet, *Rice Burn.* Courtesy of the artist. PLATE 36: Raphael Reichert, *"When I Was Your Age...."* Courtesy of the artist. PLATE 37: Michael Tompkins, *Along Highway 5.* Courtesy of Marc and Heath Schenker. Photo by Greg Kinder. PLATE 38: Fred Dalkey, *Light Rail Overcrossing.* Courtesy of the artist. PLATE 39: Robert

Else, *Workers in a Field.* Courtesy of the Solomon Dubnick Gallery, Sacramento, California. PLATE 40: Ester Hernandez, *Heroes and Saints.* Courtesy of the artist. PLATE 41: Anabelle Simon Cahn, Untitled. Courtesy of David and Diana Koeth. PLATE 42: Paul Buxman, *Orchard Along Canal.* Linder/Rempel Collection. PLATE 43: August Madrigal, *Sleeping Beauty.* Collection of Susan and Larry Early. PLATE 44: Vida Hackman, *Panorama Bluffs Burning.* Courtesy of Kenneth Hackman. The Vida and Kenneth Hackman Collection. PLATE 45: Hideo Chester Yoshida, *In the Delta.* Courtesy of the artist. PLATE 46: Harry Fonseca, *The Discovery of Gold (in California).* Courtesy of American Indian Contemporary Arts, San Francisco, California. Photo by Greg Kinder. PLATE 47: José Montoya, *The Curandera's Dog.* Courtesy of the artist. PLATE 48: Wayne Thiebaud, *River Channel.* Courtesy of Larry Evans Fine Art, Moraga, California. PLATE 49: *Topographical and Irrigation Map of the San Joaquin Valley.* Courtesy of the Shields Library, University of California, Davis. PLATE 50: *Diseño for Larkin Children's Rancho.* Courtesy of the Golden State Museum, California State Archives. PLATE 51: *Oriental Land Occupation, California.* Courtesy of the California State Library. Photo by Greg Kinder. PLATE 52: *Map of the Exploring Expedition to the Rocky Mountains.* Courtesy of the California State Library. Photo by Greg Kinder. PLATE 53: *The Sacramento Valley from the American River to Butte Creek.* Courtesy of the Shields Library, University of California, Davis. PLATE

54: *Moore's Ditch, Yolo County, California.* Courtesy of the Golden State Museum, California State Archives. PLATE 55: *Map Showing the Line and Distance of the California Pacific Railroad.* Courtesy of the Golden State Museum, California State Archives. PLATE 56: *Map of Bakersfield and Vicinity, showing Property of J. B. Haggin.* Courtesy of the California State Library. Photo by Greg Kinder. PLATE 57: *Map of Townsite of Clay.* Courtesy of the Sacramento Archives and Museum Collection Center. The Brandenberger Collection. Photos by Greg Kinder. PLATE 58: *Looking North on Unimproved McKinley Blvd.* Courtesy of the Sacramento Archives and Museum Collection Center. The Brandenberger Collection. Photo by Greg Kinder. PLATE 59: *Looking into Eucalyptus Grove.* Courtesy of the Sacramento Archives and Museum Collection Center. The Brandenberger Collection. Photo by Greg Kinder. PLATE 60: *San Joaquin County Pictorial Map.* Courtesy of The Haggin Museum; Stockton, California. Photo by Greg Kinder. PLATE 61: *Pictorial Map of Fresno County and Mid-California's Garden.* Courtesy of the California State Library. Photo by Greg Kinder. PLATE 62: *Existing and Proposed Major Water Developments in the State of California.* Courtesy of the California State Library. Photo by Greg Kinder. PLATE 63: Heath and Phoebe Schenker, *Picturing Yolo County.* Courtesy of the artists. PLATE 64: Carleton Watkins, *Artesian Well,* Courtesy of the Library of Congress, LC-USZ62-36794. PLATES 65, 66: John Pitcher Spooner, Stereographic views.

Courtesy of The Haggin Museum, Stockton, California. Photos by Dan Dion, SF. PLATE 67: *Lake View Gusher*. Courtesy of the Kern County Museum. PLATE 68: *West Sacramento Canal*. Courtesy of West Sacramento Land Company. Photo by Dan Dion, SF. PLATE 69: *New Road*. Courtesy of West Sacramento Land Company. Photo by Dan Dion, SF. PLATE 70: Frank Day Robinson, *Planting, Merced County*. Courtesy of Stephen Johnson. PLATE 71: Chester Mullen, *Diver*. Courtesy of the Shasta Historical Society. PLATE 72: Dorothea Lange, *Very Blue Eagle, Tranquility Vicinity, Fresno County*. Courtesy of the Library of Congress, LC-USF34-9850-C. PLATE 73: Ansel Adams, *Farm in the Rice Fields*. Courtesy of UCR/California Museum of Photography, University of California, Riverside. Sweeney/Rubin Ansel Adams Fiat Lux Collection. PLATE 74: Mary Swisher, *Silver Ball*. Courtesy of the artist. PLATE 75: John Pfahl, *Rancho Seco Nuclear Plant, Sacramento County, California*. Courtesy of the San Francisco Museum of Modern Art. Purchased through a gift of an anonymous donor. PLATE 76: Robert Dawson, *Large Corporate Farm*. Courtesy of the artist. PLATE 77: Stephen Johnson, *Kettleman Plain*. Courtesy of the artist. PLATE 78: Gene Kennedy, *Tree and Displaced Buildings*. Courtesy of the artist. PLATE 79: Richard Meisinger, *New American Suburbs: Young Tress and Irrigation Lines*. Courtesy of the artist. PLATE 80: David Best, *American Grafitti*. Courtesy of the artist. PLATE 81: David Robertson, *The Eyes Have It #6*. Courtesy of the

artist. Photo by Greg Kinder. PLATES 82, 83, 84, 85: Stuart Allen, *Cache Creek Levee Line; Line Drawn by a Creek; Line Drawn by a Kite; Orchard Lines*. All courtesy of the artist. PLATE 86, 87: Roman Loranc, *Living Room; San Joaquin River Slaughterhouse*. All courtesy of the artist. PLATE 88: Dugan Aguilar, *Two Worlds*. Courtesy of the artist. PLATE 89: James Fogle, *Yolo Causeway at Sunrise October 8, 1998*. Courtesy of the artist. PLATE 90: A. P. Hill, *Residence of John Wohlfrom, Yolo County*. Courtesy of the California State Library. Photo by Greg Kinder. PLATE 91: *Niederaur's Store*. From *History of Tulare County, 1883*. Courtesy of the California State Library. Photo by Greg Kinder. PLATE 92: *Ranch of Nes Hansen, Tulare Co*. From *Thompson Atlas of Tulare County, 1892*. Courtesy of the California State Library. Photo by Greg Kinder. PLATE 93: Hamilton Dale Ranch. From *Thompson Atlas of Tulare County, 1892*. Photo by Greg Kinder. PLATE 94: *Bank Building, J. Harrell, Visalia*. From *Thompson Atlas of Tulare County, 1892*. Photo by Greg Kinder. PLATE 95: Kuchel and Dresel, *Stockton*. Courtesy of The Haggin Museum, Stockton, California. Photo by Greg Kinder. PLATE 96: *Palermo Colony*. Courtesy of the California State Library. Photo by Greg Kinder. PLATE 97: Thompson and West, *Ranch of Levi Painter*. Courtesy of the California State Library. Photo by Greg Kinder. PLATE 98: N. J. Stone and Co., *Bakersfield*, Kern County. Courtesy of the California State Library. Photo by Greg Kinder. PLATE 99: *Thermalito, Home of the Orange and Olive*,

Courtesy of the California State Library. Photo by Greg Kinder. PLATES 100–102: Postcards. Courtesy of The Haggin Museum, Stockton, California. Photos by Dan Dion, SF. PLATE 103: S.P. Promotional Brochure, *California: San Joaquin Valley*. Courtesy of the California State Railroad Museum, Sacramento, California. PLATE 104: S.P. Promotional Brochure, *California: Sacramento Valley*. Courtesy of the California State Railroad Museum, Sacramento, California. PLATE 105: Map of the Netherlands Route. Courtesy of the California State Railroad Museum, Sacramento, California. PLATE 106: Borough, S.P. Poster: *The Netherlands Route*. Courtesy of the California State Railroad Museum, Sacramento, California. PLATES 107–108: County Promotional Pamphlets. Courtesy of The Haggin Museum, Stockton, California. Photos by Greg Kinder. PLATE 109: *Gateway Magazine*. Courtesy of The Haggin Museum, Stockton, California. Photo by Greg Kinder. PLATES 110–112: Ralph Yardley, Do You Remember cartoons. Courtesy of The Haggin Museum, Stockton, California. Gift of the *Stockton Record*. PLATES 113–114: Crate Labels. Courtesy of the Shields Library, University of California, Davis. Special Collections.